UNCLEAN FOODS
To Eat or Not To Eat

Glen Striemer

TEACH Services, Inc.
PUBLISHING
www.TEACHServices.com • (800) 367-1844

World rights reserved. This book or any portion thereof may not be copied or reproduced in any form or manner whatever, except as provided by law, without the written permission of the publisher, except by a reviewer who may quote brief passages in a review.

The author assumes full responsibility for the accuracy and interpretation of the Ellen White quotations cited in this book. Unless otherwise indicated, all scripture quotations are taken from the King James Version of the Bible.

The ESV® Bible (The Holy Bible, English Standard Version®). ESV® Text Edition: 2016. Copyright © 2001 by Crossway, a publishing ministry of Good News Publishers. The ESV® text has been reproduced in cooperation with and by permission of Good News Publishers. Unauthorized reproduction of this publication is prohibited. All rights reserved.

Copyright © 2019 Glen Striemer

Copyright © 2019 TEACH Services, Inc.

ISBN-13: 978-1-4796-0924-6 (Paperback)

ISBN-13: 978-1-4796-0925-3 (ePub)

Library of Congress Control Number: 2018956439

Scripture quotations marked The Message are taken from The Message. Copyright © 1993, 1994, 1995, 1996, 2000, 2001, 2002. Used by permission of NavPress Publishing Group.

Scripture quotations marked NASB are taken from the New American Standard Bible®, copyright © 1960, 1962, 1963, 1968, 1971, 1972, 1973, 1975, 1977, 1995 by The Lockman Foundation. Used by permission.

Scripture quotations marked NIV are taken from The Holy Bible, New International Version®, NIV®. Copyright © 1973, 1978, 1984, 2011 by Biblica, Inc.™ Used by permission. All rights reserved world wide.

Texts credited to NKJV are taken from the New King James Version®. Copyright © 1982 by Thomas Nelson, Inc. Used by permission. All rights reserved.

Scripture quotations marked NLT are taken from the Holy Bible, New Living Translation, copyright © 1996, 2004, 2007 by Tyndale House Foundation. Used by permission of Tyndale House Publishers, Inc., Carol Stream, Illinois 60188. All rights reserved.

Scripture quotations marked REB are taken from The Revised English Bible, copyright © Cambridge University Press and Oxford University Press 1989. All rights reserved.

www.TEACHServices.com • (800) 367-1844

Table of Contents

Introduction v

Dietary Laws 1

Old Testament Prophets 14

Jesus and Disciples 20

At the Cross 28

Peter's Vision 33

Jerusalem Council AD 51 37

Idol Worship 43

Apostle Paul and Idol Foods 58

Paul Challenges Corinthians 65

New Testament Prophecy 78

None of These Diseases 81

Introduction

CLEAN AND UNCLEAN ANIMALS

Prior to the flood there appeared no recorded instruction from God to divide animals into clean and unclean as permission to eat flesh foods had never been granted. The wicked Antediluvian race delighted in destroying the life of animals and the use of flesh food rendered them cruel and bloodthirsty. As the Antediluvian Age neared its final conclusion, there came a command from God far different from any instruction mankind had ever received:

"Of every clean beast thou shalt take to thee by sevens, the male and his female: and of beasts that are not clean by two, the male and his female" (Gen. 7:2).

Many Bible translations say the clean animals came in seven pairs but a sensible conclusion is that one male and six females made up the seven. Any farmer knows it would have made for a more peaceful ark.

God's land and air creatures were divided into two groups, clean and unclean. The Lord, who directed in minute details construction of an ark able to withstand the furious destruction of the world, must also have explained in detail to Noah what He meant by clean and unclean in regard to food. Aboard the ark were single pairs of unclean species, one male and one female, in order that they may reproduce and replenish the earth. Had the passengers eaten the *unclean* animals, it would have meant the extinction of a species. When the ark finally found dry land, sacrifices were made, and animals were eaten to survive in a new, barren world void of food stocks.

This clear command by God to Noah regarding clean and unclean animals eliminates the theory that the laws of Moses were the *Jewish laws.* Of the eight surviving members of the ancient world, the Jews had not yet been born! Abraham was many generations removed from Noah's son Shem, his direct ancestor who was on the boat.

Some Christians conclude because God's command to Noah did not include fish, nor specify unclean birds, that it was only a law regarding animal sacrifices. However, certain Bible translations state the obvious implication this verbal dietary law included all creatures designated for eating:

"Take with you seven pairs—male and female—*of each animal I have approved for eating* **and for sacrifice, and take one pair of each of the others"** (Gen. 7:2, New Living Translation; emphasis added).

As for the birds, after the Flood, **"Noah ... took of every clean beast, and of every clean fowl, and offered burnt offerings"** (Gen. 8:20).

After the flood everything had been destroyed upon which man could survive. The dove sent forth from the ark was fortunate to find a single leaf. God could have chosen this point in history to introduce manna to feed the eight remaining souls but instead the Lord gave Noah permission to eat of the clean animals which had been taken upon the ark.

Clean animals such as lambs, goats, and bulls were sacrificed, but there are clean animals mentioned in the dietary laws of Moses that were never used as sacrifices to God. If the purpose of God's command was for sacrifices only then God would have told Noah to take only sheep, cattle, and goats in sevens. But God gave Noah permission to kill and eat animal flesh immediately after the deluge, proving the excessive clean animals were primarily to be used as food for mankind.

Because of the devastating effect the raging waters would have had washing the top soil away, Noah and his family would have to live a season without fruit and vegetables. Although they took a good supply aboard the ark, it would probably not be enough to sustain them until they were able to plant and harvest a crop. During this time of transition the extra pairs of clean animals would supply this food. When the boat landed and the dove found only a leaf to eat, Noah's crew knew what God meant by clean and unclean. It was time to eat flesh or perish.

The surviving creatures knew things had changed as well. In post-flood times, God now declares the clean animals of this earth would be in perpetual danger from man who will be allowed to eat them for food:

"And the fear of you and the dread of you shall be on every beast of the earth, on every bird of the air, on all that move on the earth, and on all the fish of the sea. They are given into your hand.

Every moving thing that liveth shall be meat for you; even as the green herb have I given you all things" (Gen. 9:1–3).

This verse does not say that every living, breathing creature is clean and fit to eat. God did not give poisonous herbs as food. He gave man the healthful herbs.

Just as every green plant that God caused to grow out of the ground was not designed for food, so it is with animal flesh. Man can determine which herbs are healthful, but man cannot by himself determine which flesh foods are harmful. God determined for Noah which foods were clean and gave us in His printed Word which meats are clean.

Since the flood, every clean, healthful, non-poisonous type of animal life is allowed for food. Circumstances had changed from every living creature eating green herbs, to man now eating every living thing.

During the Exodus from Egypt, God sent heavenly manna to feed the people for forty years. Upon the Jewish settlement in Canaan, the Israelites were permitted the use of animal food, but under careful restrictions. It was here that clean and unclean foods were repeated to Moses to relay to the people.

After the restoration of all things spoken of by the prophets, animals will not eat each other in heaven. **"The wolf also shall dwell with the lamb, and the leopard shall lie down with the kid; and the calf and the young lion and the fatling together; and a little child shall lead them. And the cow and the bear shall feed; their young ones shall lie down together: and the lion shall eat straw like the ox ... They shall not hurt nor destroy in all my holy mountain"** (Isa. 11:6, 7).

In heaven there is no need of clean or unclean animals being eaten for there will be no killing.

Dietary Laws

During Egyptian captivity the Jews were heavily into the fleshpots of Egypt. After the Exodus, God added a myriad of stipulations regarding the sacrificial system, each one designed to point to Christ. The spiritual application of Jesus the Lamb could finally be seen again. Likewise, the simple command to eat the clean and leave the unclean was not sufficient for such a backslidden people coming out of four generations of servitude to an Egyptian lifestyle. The Lord added multiple and minute regulations to ensure the health of the Jewish nation. God's audible law of health, last stated so simply to Noah, had now become complex through necessity. Eventually, the Jews added man-made laws on top of God's dietary laws which had been given to them.

Unlike any previous era, God was dealing with upwards of two million refugees heading out from Egypt into the hot desert sun where water was scarce. God's health laws were strict, precise, and designed to prevent plagues in the camp. The principles of healthy living established by the laws of Moses have stood the test of time. Much loss of life would have been spared in the Middle Ages and beyond had medical practitioners followed the wise counsel given Moses on sanitation. Too many centuries passed, resulting in much loss of life, before washing hands after operations or autopsies became standard medical practice.

To the Jews, the dietary restrictions given by God were both spiritual and physical in nature. *"These laws have been given for justice' sake to awake pious thoughts and to form the character ... All these things are forbidden, because they deprave the blood and make it susceptible to many diseases; they pollute the body and the soul ... The unclean animals cause coarseness and dullness of the soul"* (Arama).

The Jews claim Christians base their eating patterns upon desires rather than the Word of God. The primary calling of many unclean animals is to act as vital sanitation workers in our ecology. If left to determine which animals were clean by sight and habits, then a rabbit would be cleanest of all, while a chicken would appear to be dirty.

In some South American countries, people sit at a table with a hole in its center. The purpose of the hole is to hold the head of a live monkey above the table. Those partaking of this delicacy must strike the monkey's head with a hammer until its brains are exposed. They then eat the fresh brains. This is probably nauseating to some, but it helps give us a clearer picture of how diets differ culturally. Asians eat mice but would never eat an oyster which they find disgusting. Americans reverse these practices to suit their culture. It is all in the eye of the beholder and to depend on one's culture norms as a rule of diet is to depend upon the heart of man and we know where that usually leads. It is not inherently in man to know which animals are clean to eat. Without the Holy Scriptures we would have no way of knowing.

"For I am the Lord your God: ye shall therefore sanctify yourselves, and ye shall be holy; for I am holy ... This is the law of the beasts, and of the fowl, and of every living creature that moveth in the waters, and of every creature that creepeth upon the earth: To make a difference between the clean, and between the beast that may be eaten and the beast that may not be eaten" (Lev. 11:44–47).

"And the Lord spake unto Moses and to Aaron, saying unto them, 'Speak unto the children of Israel, saying These are the beasts which ye shall eat among all the beasts that are on the earth'" (Lev. 11:2).

ANIMALS

"Whatsoever parteth the hoof, and is clovenfooted, and cheweth the cud, among the beasts, that ye shall eat. And every beast that parteth the hoof, and cleaveth the cleft into two claws, and cheweth the cud among the beasts, that shall ye eat" (Deut. 14:6).

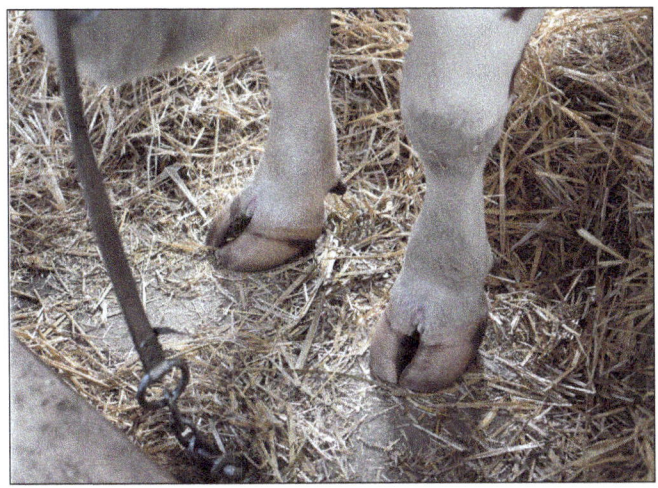

PARTETH THE HOOF

The ancient Jews looked upon the parted hoof as symbolic of how that people perceives itself. The parted hoof represents the duality of life. From the beginning of existence, Judaism has celebrated duality: land/heavens, light/darkness, humanity/God, Isaac/Ishmael, Jacob/Esau, Shabbat/the workday week, holy/profane. The parted hoof is the symbol of their sense of life. There is division in the world—a division that will not be healed until the days of their coming Jewish Messiah. As Christians, we are separated from the literal fellowship of Christ our Elder Brother, thus the parted hoof could symbolically point to this parting, until we reunite at the great banquet feast in heaven where clean and unclean will no longer be an issue in a land without killing.

CHEW THE CUD

Cud is a portion of food that returns from a ruminant's stomach to the mouth, where it is chewed for a second time. It is a bolus of semi-degraded food which is regurgitated. To the ancient Jews, chewing the cud represented a learning experience.

> *"Just as a cud-chewing animal after biting through the food keeps it at rest in the gullet, after a bit again draws it up and chews it and then passes it on to the belly, so the student, after receiving from the teacher the principles and lore of wisdom, prolongs the process of learning, since he cannot at once comprehend and grasp them securely, until,*

by using memory to call up each thing that he has heard ... he stamps a firm impression of them on his soul." (Special Laws, 4:106–107)

Jews are those who take wisdom and cogitate upon it and bring it back up again and chew on it, never happy with what they have learned, always looking for a way to comprehend it and to refine it.

The dictionary definition of ruminate is:

1. chew the cud; grip or tear with teeth; chew; chomp; crush; gnaw; masticate; nibble.

2. Meditate; muse; ponder; reflect; brainstorm; brood; contemplate; rack one's brains; stew about.

The popular expression *"chewing one's cud"* signifies meditating or pondering a thought.

Clean animals are herbivores, eating plants which are thoroughly digested and fermented. They have a stomach divided into multiple sacs for fermentation of plant foods consumed. This complex gastric system chemically disinfects food before it passes to the intestine and into the bloodstream.

EAT

Antelope, bison, caribou, cattle, gazelle, deer, elk, goat, hart, moose, oxen, pronghorn, reindeer, sheep, water buffalo, yak.

A class of animal life may have existed in the days of Moses which are now extinct such as the unicorn, which is mentioned six times in Scripture.

DON'T EAT

Apes, armadillo, badger, bear, beaver, boar, camels, cat, cheetah, coyote, dog, donkey, elephant, ferret, fox, giraffe, gorilla, groundhog, hare, hedgehog, hippopotamus, horse, hyena, jackal, jaguar, kangaroo, koala, kookaburra, leopard, lion, llama, lynx, mole, monkey, mouse, mule, muskrat, opossum, panther, pigs, porcupine, rabbit, raccoon, rat, rhino, skunk, slug, squirrel, tiger, wallaby, weasel, wolf, wolverine, wombat, zebra.

God forbids the consumption of scavengers and carrion eaters, which devour other animals for their food and thrive on decaying flesh. They are predatory in nature, often preying on the weakest and diseased. They consume flesh that would sicken or kill a human.

The unclean animals are omnivore (carnivore diet of flesh). They have a single sac stomach in which no fermentation takes place. Humans have a single sac stomach.

Fermentation of flesh normally takes place in the final section of the digestive track.

"Nevertheless, these shall ye not eat of them that chew the cud, or of them that divide the hoof ... of their flesh shall ye not eat ... they are unclean unto you" (Lev. 11: 4–8).

"And whatsoever goeth upon his paws, among all manner of beasts that go on all four, those are unclean unto you" (Lev. 11:27).

FISH

"These shall ye eat of all that are in the waters: whatsoever hath fins and scales in the waters, in the seas, and in the rivers, them shall ye eat" (Lev. 11:9).

Sub-species of fish possessing fins and scales are practically endless.

EAT

Anchovy, angelfish, ballyhoo, barracuda, bass, bigeyes, blackfish, blacksmith, blueback, bluefish, bluegill, boccaccio, bonefish, bonitos, bowfin, brill, butterfish, cabrilla, carp, chub, cichlids, cod, coho, crappie, croaker, cunner, damselfishes, darter, doctor fish, drum, flounder, flying fishes, frost fish, gaby, goatfishes, gobies, gold eye, goldfish, grayling, greenlings, groupers, grunts, hake, halibut, hardtail, hawk fishes, herring, hogfish, jack, john dory, kelpfish, ladyfish, lizardfishes, mackerel, menhaden, milkfish, minnow, mojarras, mullet, muskellunge, needlefish, parrotfish, patagonian tooth fish, perch, pig fish, pike, pollack, pomfret, pompano, porgy, redfish, rockfish, rosefish, sablefish, salmon, sardine, sargeant, sea robins, shad, sheepshead, silversides, skipjack, smelt, snapper, snook, spadefish, squirrelfishes, sole, steelhead, sucker, sunfish, surgeon fish, tarpon, tripletale, trout, tuna, turbot, wahoo, weakfish, whitefish, whiting, wrasses.

DON'T EAT

"And all that have not fins and scales in the seas, and in the rivers, of all that move in the waters, and of any living thing which is in the waters, they shall be an abomination unto you" (Lev. 11:10).

Abalone, billfishes, blowfish, bullhead, burbot, catfish, caviar, clam, crab, crayfish, cutlass, cuttlefish, dogfish, dolphin, eel, goosefish, grayfish, jellyfish, kingfish, lamprey, leatherjacket, limpet, lobster, lumpfish, marlin, monkfish, mussel, ocean pout, octopus, oilfish, otter, oyster, paddlefish, porpoise, prawn, rays, rock prickle back, sailfish, sand lances, sawfish, scallop, sculpins, seal, shark, shrimp, skates, slug, snail, squid, stickleback, sturgeon, swordfish, toadfish, triggerfish, trunkfish, turbot, walrus, whale, wolfish.

A class of unclean marine life may have existed in the days of Moses who are now extinct like the leviathan, the giant sea creature mentioned in the Book of Job, Psalms, and Isaiah.

The Jews look upon fishes without fins and scales, which stay in the deep water, and especially those in swampy water, as possessing a degree of cold and humidity which acts mortally. Christians should be as wise when it comes to devouring God's appointed pollution control devices which inhabit the murky lower portion of the waters. Bottom dwellers scavenge for dead animals on the sea floor, consuming decaying matter, including sewage.

BIRDS

In regard to the fowl that are clean, it is more a case of determining which types of fowl are unclean. As a rule of thumb, birds of prey and most water fowl are unclean. Moses is specific about which birds are unclean while mentioning only eating clean birds after their kind. Nonetheless, from the various types of unclean birds we determine which feathered creatures are clean. Clean birds generally have a craw and double-skinned stomach, an elongated middle, hind toe, and a gizzard.

The Jews see spiritual aspects in the eating of birds. "It is especially emphasized that birds of prey have been forbidden, to teach that man shall practise justice; and not, depending upon his own strength, do injury to others" (*The Jewish Encyclopedia*). Birds of prey have a marked inclination to cruelty.

EAT

"Of all clean birds ye shall eat ... All clean fowls ye may eat" (Deut. 14:11, 20).

Chicken, grouse, pigeon, dove, guinea fowl, partridge, quail, turkey, pheasant.

DON'T EAT

"And these are they which ye shall have in abomination among the fowls; they shall not be eaten…" (Lev. 11:13).

Albatross, bat, bittern, buzzard, condor, coot, cormorant, crane, crow, cuckoo, eagle, emu, flamingo, grebe, grosbeak, gull, hawk, heron, kite, lapwing, loon, magpie, osprey, ostrich, owl, parrot, pelican, penguin, plover, rail, raven, roadrunner, sandpiper, seagull, sparrow, stork, swallow, swift, vulture, water hen, woodpecker.

"... all fowls that creep, going on all four" (Lev. 11:20).

There are three distinct possibilities regarding this class of unclean fowl:

(1) "The bat has claws attached to its leathern wings, which serve in place of feet to crawl by, the feet and legs not being distinct" *(Adam Clarke's Commentaries).*

Note: Some scientists claim the Bible as being false because bats are not birds, but if God wishes to place bats in with the birds that is fine with us.

(2) Creatures who do not exist except in rare mutations. "Degenerate from their proper nature, and are of a mongrel kind, which may intimate that apostates in religion are abominable" *(John Wesley's Commentary).*

> *It is estimated that in our lifetime we will consume upwards of one pound of insects through food harvesting and processing gaffs*

(3) The KJV translators may have inserted the word "fowl" incorrectly. The New American Standard, New International, American Standard, Douey, Darby, English Revised, Webster's Bible, World English, Young's Literal Translation, and Bible Lexicon, all substitute insects in place of the word fowl as used in these verses in the KJV.

CREATURES IN QUESTION

Certain birds are in dispute, even among the Jews as to what can or cannot be eaten. We take the position, better to play it safe than sorry. Birds in question as to whether they are clean are: ducks, goose, and swan, for the simple reason that clean birds are foragers while this kind are bottom feeders with webbed feet containing much more fat.

For example, a roasted duck contains 25g. of fat compared to 3g. of fat for chicken.

Some large tuna, with their plastic-type skin, are also questionable when discerning whether they possess smooth skin or scales.

INSECTS

Entomophagy is the act of eating insects as a food. The thought of eating insects is revolting to us, but it is estimated that in our lifetime we will consume upwards of one pound of insects through food harvesting and processing gaffs.

Fried insects are a delicacy in China, as well as giant water bugs. Many African, Asian, Latin American, and Australian societies consider insects as a valuable source of protein, vitamins, and minerals. In India, the many tribal groups eat ants as well as locust, which are also a South Korean delicacy. Mexicans purchase caterpillars sold fresh in the markets then fry them before eating. The goliath beetle, an African favorite, grows to five inches. Silkworm pupae and ant eggs are the African norm. In Thailand, crickets are considered one of the best tasting insects. They are cooked and served as crunchy snacks as well as hard shell beetles. In Asia, wild bees are so heavily hunted that farmers are considering raising them for food to avoid their extinction.

Flying insects are fried after removing their wings and legs, and beetles and larvae add variety to everyday meals. Many of the insects eaten are those which can be gathered in large numbers such as ants, termites, and grasshoppers. Termites, especially the large queen castles, where a single termite can measure three inches long, are considered a better source of protein than beef, and are manufactured into cooking oil. Locusts are gathered in the morning before they are active, then boiled, cleaned, and salted. Poisonous scorpions are often fried impaled on a stick and believed to possess healing properties.

Some cultures add fried silkworms to the list of healing foods. When eating cicadas (cricket) one is counseled to avoid wings and legs getting stuck in your teeth. Even centipedes are eaten for healing. And let us not forget the popular school library book that grossed out a generation of children, *How To Eat Fried Worms*.

In developed countries, armed forces eat certain insects as part of survival training. There are 1,462 recorded species of edible insects.

Many Jewish communities have lost interest in eating clean insects. Today's rabbis are uncertain as to which insects were specifically permitted, so now all insects in European Jewish society are prohibited.

"Yet, these may ye eat of every flying creeping thing that goeth upon all four, which have legs above their feet, to leap withal upon the earth" (Lev 11:21).

EAT

Beetle, crickets, grasshoppers, locust.
"John the Baptist ... his meat was locusts and wild honey" (Matt. 3:4).

Bees' honey is, however, considered clean because the honey is not made by bees, but is rather collected nectar and concentrated by bees.

DON'T EAT

Centipedes, spiders, snail, worm, and an untold number of other creeping things which we leave to insect eating societies to figure out for themselves what is clean.

"These also shall be unclean unto you among the creeping things that creep upon the earth ... all other flying creeping things, which have four feet ... And every creeping thing that creepeth upon the earth ... it shall not be eaten. Whatsoever ... goeth upon all four, or whatsoever hath more feet among all creeping things that creep upon the earth, them ye shall not eat ... And every creeping thing that flieth is unclean unto you: they shall not be eaten." (Lev. 11:23, 29, 41, 42; Deut. 14:19)

REPTILES

"Whatsoever goeth upon the belly ... them shall ye not eat…" (Deut. 14:42).

DO NOT EAT

Alligators, caiman, chameleon, crocodiles, gecko, lizards, iguana, monitor, snakes, turtles.

In the case of reptiles and amphibians, there are no clean creatures available to eat, thus there is no confusion as to what is clean and what is not.

AMPHIBIANS

DO NOT EAT

Blindworm, frog, mantella, newt, salamander, toad.

Some Christian churches follow the dietary laws, most notable the Seventh-day Adventists, who do not adhere to keeping the Old Covenant feast days, and those churches who have reverted to keeping the feast days.

Some extreme Jewish mystics *[Kabbalah]* believe that at the coming of their Messiah, all will become purer and nobler and unclean animals will then be permitted as food.

ABOMINATIONS

All abominations come under one Satanic leader in the form of the 666 Antichrist, and it has been this way since the beginning of time:

"Having a golden cup in her hand full of abominations and filthiness of her fornication: And upon her forehead was a name written, MYSTERY, BABYLON THE GREAT, THE MOTHER OF HARLOTS AND ABOMINATIONS OF THE EARTH" (Rev. 17:4, 5; emphasis added).

The Bible dictionary describes an abomination as *"the object of abhorrence."* Men who commit **"every abomination to the Lord, which He hateth ...Thou shalt not do so"** (Deut. 12:31).

"Thou shalt not eat any abominable thing" (Deut. 14:3).

"And all that have not fins and scales ... of any living thing which is in the waters, they shall be an abomination unto you ... (Lev. 11:10).

"And these are they which ye shall have in abomination among the fowls; they shall not be eaten ..." (Lev. 11:13).

"Whatsoever goeth upon the belly ... them shall ye not eat, for they are an abomination" (Deut. 14:42).

Eating unclean foods is not simply a test of obedience like that given Adam and Eve. God's principles of health demand that whosoever partakes of abominable food will suffer because of it. Why tempt ye the Lord God when it comes to eating unclean foods which He classed as being abominations?

BAAL WORSHIP

Vile are the company of guests who dine at the table of spiritual abominations. Heading the list of other abominations are those who worship idols: **"Every abomination ... hath they done ... even their sons and daughters they have burnt in the fire to their gods"** (Deut. 12:31).

Dietary Laws ♦ 11

This wickedness exhibited by the pagan nations soon worked its way into the worship of the nation of promise: *"And they built the house places of Baal ... to cause their sons and their daughters to pass through the fire unto Molech; which I commanded them not, neither came it into My mind, that they should do this abomination, to cause Judah to sin"* (Jer. 32:35).

"The graven images of their gods shall ye burn with fire: thou shalt not desire the silver or gold that is on them, nor take it unto thee, lest thou be snared therein: for it is an abomination to the Lord thy God. Neither shalt thou bring an abomination into thine house, lest thou be a cursed thing like it: but thou shalt utterly detest it, and thou shalt utterly abhor it; for it is a cursed thing" (Deut. 7:25, 26).

"Cursed be the man that maketh any graven or molten image, an abomination unto the Lord, the work of the hands of the craftsman, and putteth it in a secret place" (Deut. 27:15).

OCCULTISM

Pantheism, astrology and the occult are grouped together as abominations: *"If there be found any among you ... and hath gone and served other gods, and worshipped them, either the sun, or moon, or any of the host of heaven ... that such an abomination is wrought in Israel ... shalt stone them with stones till they die"* (Deut. 17:2–4).

"There shall not be found among you any one ... that useth divination, or an observer of times, or an enchanter, or a witch, or a charmer, or a consulter with familiar spirits, or a wizard, or a necromancer. For all that do these things are an abomination unto the Lord: and because of these abominations the Lord thy God doth drive them out before thee" (Deut. 18:10–12).

IMMORALITY

It is no surprise that perverse sexual immorality is high on the list of abominations, including a long trail of incestuous behavior and bestiality that we choose not to mention here:

"... Moreover, thou shalt not lie carnally with thy neighbour's wife ... thou shalt not lie with mankind as with womankind—it is an abomination ... for all these abominations have the men of the land done ... for whosoever shall commit any of these abominations, even the souls that commit them shall be cut off ..." (Lev. 18:6–30).

"Thou shalt not bring the hire of a whore ... into the house of the Lord thy God for any vow ... an abomination ..." (Deut. 23:18).

"Judah hath dealt treacherously, and an abomination is committed in Israel ... for Judah hath profaned the holiness of the Lord which he loved, and hath married the daughter of a strange god" (Mal. 2:11). "And there shall in no wise enter into [heaven] any thing that defileth, neither whatsoever worketh abomination ..." (Rev. 21:27).

SELF-RIGHTEOUSNESS

God takes very seriously the spirit of sacrifice that we bring unto Him. In Isaiah's day it reached its peak with professors of religion making a mockery of the entire sacrificial system:

"Bring no more vain oblations; incense is an abomination unto Me ... your new moons and appointed feasts My soul hateth ... I am weary to bear them" (Isa. 1:13, 14).

"The sacrifice of the wicked is an abomination: how much more when he bringeth it with a wicked mind?" (Prov. 21:27).

"I brought you into a plentiful country, to eat the fruit thereof and the goodness thereof; but when ye entered; ye defiled my land and made Mine heritage an abomination" (Jer. 2:7).

Jesus spoke boldly to the priesthood of Pharisees who continually derided Him:

"Ye are they which justify yourselves before men; but God knoweth your hearts: for that which is highly esteemed among men is abomination in the sight of God" (Luke 16:15).

God warns the backsliders the eternal results of practicing abominations: "But when the righteous turneth away from his righteousness, and committeth iniquity, and doeth according to all the abominations that the wicked man doeth, shall he live?" (Ezek. 18:24).

CORRUPTION

The Lord groups mean-spirited business practices and the charging of monetary interest (usury) to believers as an abomination in His sight: "Hath given forth upon usury, and hath taken increase ... hath oppressed the poor and needy ... hath not restored the pledge ... hath committed abominations" (Ezek. 18:12, 13).

"Thou shalt have a perfect and just weight, a perfect and just measure shalt thou have ... thou shalt not have in thine house divers measures ... for all that do such things ... are an abomination unto the Lord thy God" (Deut. 25:14–16).

STUBBORNESS

Is the abominable pig, a relied source of income for some, and a culinary delight for others, worth this risk? The Bible calls swine an abomination and nothing else. There is not one cuddly, affectionate reference to it from Genesis to Revelation.

Never has a spiritual abomination moved out of the sin category and into the approved norm of behavior. Are we to surmise that the physical abominations of food deserve a separate classification apart from the spiritual? For what earthly purpose would Jesus suddenly clean up abominable food? Was it decided we need to eat unclean foods in order to be healthier?

LAST DAYS

The Lord in His mercy has winked at the ignorance of Christians in relation to the eating of foods God calls abominable. The day will come however, when this time of ignorance is past. If you believe the imminent return of Jesus is nigh at the doors, then heed these verses:

"Were they ashamed when they had committed abomination? Nay, they were not at all ashamed, neither could they blush ... at that time I visit them they shall be cast down, saith the Lord" (Jer. 6:15).

"And the Lord said unto him, Go through the midst of the city, through the midst of Jerusalem, and set a mark upon the foreheads of the men that sigh and cry for all the abominations that be done in the midst thereof ... Slay utterly old and young, both maids and little children, and women: but come not near any man upon whom is the mark; and begin at my sanctuary" (Ezek. 9:4–6).

If we truly believe, then we should accept—that an abomination was always an abomination, and will continue to be an abomination, when the end finally comes with Jesus riding into view of the saints.

Old Testament Prophets

ISAIAH

The prophet Isaiah, looking down to Jesus' day and beyond, penned these inspired words: **"Then the eyes of the blind shall be opened, and the ears of the deaf shall be unstopped. Then shall the lame man leap as an hart, and the tongue of the dumb sing ... And an highway shall be there, and a Way, and it shall be called the Way of holiness; the unclean shall not pass over it ... but the redeemed shall walk there"** (Isa. 35:8–9).

Jesus fulfilled this prophecy. Among the differing ways to become unclean, none were as brash as eating the abominable foods. People who knowingly ate forbidden foods were called unclean. They were not going to walk with Jesus—not now, nor in heaven.

"I have spread out My hands all the day unto a rebellious people, which walketh in a way that was not good, after their own thoughts; A people that provoketh Me to anger continually to My face ... which eat swine's flesh, and broth of abominable things is in their vessels; which say ... I am holier than Thou" (Isa. 65:2–5).

God angrily rebukes a rebellious band of legalists, a people who eat unclean foods. What could make God **"Who changeth not"** sanction eating swine's flesh and broth of abominable things to the place where it would be called good? It is the work of sorts who walk after their own thoughts.

"For, behold, the Lord will come with fire, and with His chariots like a whirlwind, to render His anger with fury, and His rebuke with flames of fire" (Isa. 66:15). Every Bible Commentary we read links these verses of Isaiah 66 to the second coming of Jesus.

"For by fire and by His sword will the Lord plead with all flesh: and the slain of the Lord shall be many" (Isa. 66:16).

It is not God's will that any should perish. In Isaiah we foresee a picture of the last hours before probation closes on mankind. God pleads with fire, which in prophecy represents the Holy Ghost. The mighty Spirit is wooing the rebellious ones to repent before it is too late. The sword represents the Word of God clearly pointing out the things which need to be repented of. The slain of the Lord may represent those who are slain in the Spirit of the Lord, men who are given one last chance.

"They that sanctify themselves, and purify themselves in the gardens behind one tree in the midst, eating swine's flesh, and the abomination, and the mouse, shall be consumed together, saith the Lord" (Isa. 66: 15–17).

Isaiah prophesies of those who are eating unclean foods at the Second Coming. Did the angel who gave Isaiah the vision forget that after the Cross you could eat unclean foods? Did Isaiah copy this vision incorrectly? Did Bible Scholars who selected passages for inclusion in the canon, err by including this series of texts? No! All Scripture is given by inspiration. Of greater importance is the link between sanctifying oneself (righteousness by works) and the rebellion of eating unclean foods. **"As many as I love, I rebuke and chasten: be zealous therefore, and repent"** (Rev. 3:19).

> *Christians in this last hour can either be consumed by the Lord in truth and repentance or be consumed in the end by fire*

Christians in this last hour can either be consumed by the Lord in truth and repentance or be consumed in the end by fire.

Adam and Eve forever threw mankind into sin because of rebellious disobedience involving food. Nothing has changed. With the temptation of the fleshpot before him, man is given a final choice—serve ye this day whom ye will—be it the Lord with clean, pure foods, or the devil with the unclean. Eating unclean abominable foods, against God's direct counsel represents the rebellious spirit of Satan's followers. The unclean fleshpots appear to be the final test of which spirit rules the day.

Is eating unclean meat a *spiritual sin?* It may defile the health of a man, but not affect his eternal state as long as the man is ignorant of God's requirements. However, if one understands the command in diet as coming from their Creator, then rejects it, that person is accountable and in danger of judgment due to open rebellion. Keeping Isaiah's last day prophecy in mind helps our perspective as we read the desperate interpretations of scholars to fulfill the carnal nature and sanction the use of unclean foods in the New Testament.

"He that offered an oblation, as if he offered swine's blood … Yea, they have chosen their own ways, and their soul delighted in their abominations" (Isa. 66:3). The pattern is too strong to ignore—eating unclean foods is always tied to rebellion, choosing man's way over God's way. **"The heart is deceitful above all things, and desperately wicked: who can know it?"** (Jer. 17:9).

EZEKIEL

"Ah, Lord God! Behold my soul hath not been polluted: for from my youth up even till now ... neither came there abominable flesh into my mouth" (Ezek. 4:14).

So much for weak arguments from some that Noah was allowed to eat unclean foods and Old Testament characters followed suit. God's prophets, late into the Old Testament were adhering to the dietary laws of Moses.

"Her priests have violated My law, and have profaned Mine holy things: they have put no difference between the holy and the profane, neither have they shewed difference between the clean and the unclean ... and I am profaned among them" (Ezek. 22:26).

Shepherds, as leaders of the flock, are called into question here. Many modern pastors have placed no difference between clean and unclean, thus leading entire flocks astray.

"And they shall teach My people the difference between the holy and the profane, and cause them to discern between the unclean and the clean" (Ezek. 44:23).

This is the true role of any pastor, to rightly divide the word of truth and lead his charge into righteousness.

DANIEL IN BABYLON

There is evidence in the Bible that a wholesome diet offers immediate health benefits. This experiment of diet took place a thousand years after God had given Moses the dietary laws.

In 607 BC **"Came Nebuchadnezzar king of Babylon unto Jerusalem and besieged it"** (Dan. 1:1). Why did the Lord **"... take all the families of the north ..."** then call Nebuchadnezzar **"My servant"** for bringing His chosen people into captivity? (Jer. 25:9). To the kingdom of Judah came these solemn words: **"The Lord hath sent unto you all His servants the prophets ... but ye have not hearkened ... Go not after other gods to serve them, and to worship them ..."** (Jer. 25: 4–6).

From out of this sorry rabble of rebellious Jews, the king found four faithful Hebrews: **"Children in whom was no blemish, but well favored, and skilful in all wisdom, and cunning in knowledge, and understanding science, and such as had ability in them to stand in the king's palace, and whom they might teach the learning and the tongue of the Chaldeans"** (Dan. 1:4).

Nebuchadnezzar had special plans for these four youths to help run his global empire. The plan consisted of gradually morphing idol worship into their lives. Nebuchadnezzar began by insulting the four worthies with new names designed to undermine their Hebrew heritage and glorify the gods of Babylon (Dan. 1:7). Daniel, *"God is my judge,"* became Belteshazzar, prince of the treasures of Bel, or Baal.

Hananiah, *"Gift of gracious God,"* became Shadrach (illumined by the sun god Shamash).

Mishael, *"Who is like God,"* became Meshach, exalting Ishtar, queen of heaven.

Azariah, *"Help of God,"* became Abed-nego, slave of Nebo, god of wisdom and education.

"And the king appointed them a daily provision of the king's meat ... But Daniel purposed in his heart that he would not defile himself with the portion of the king's meat ... therefore he requested of the prince of the eunuchs that he might not defile himself" (Dan. 1:5, 7). The first instance of defilement found in the Bible is found when God commands His children not to eat unclean foods lest ye be defiled (Lev. 11:44). We can only conclude that Daniel, Hananiah, Mishael, and Azariah refused unclean foods presented to them by King Nebuchadnezzar.

To examine a long list of defilements in the Bible forms a despicable list of sins which block entrance into heaven. Eating foods sacrificed to idols also falls in with this class. Are we to believe that Jesus later extracted the unclean foods from the defilement group and strangely cleansed them for eating, while all other defilements remain worthy of condemnation unto eternal death?

Daniel made a special request: **"Give us pulse [vegetables] to eat, and water to drink"** (Dan. 1:12). This semi-fast of vegetables and water was in stark contrast to eating the king's prescribed greasy meats and fermented wines. The result was conclusive: **"At the end of ten days their countenances appeared fairer and fatter in flesh than all the children which did eat the portion of the king's meat"** (Dan. 1:15).

Daniel did not purposely launch a campaign for vegetarianism, nor did he refuse the food strictly for health reasons. With the Babylonian king it was all about idol worship, no different than heathen kings before or after him. With captive Israel Nebuchadnezzar found a population willing to comply with his desires for idol worship especially under threat of harm. This was witnessed when the entire captive nation, with the exception of the Hebrew worthies, bowed down to the golden image.

These Hebrew worthies were God's representatives, men who were as true as steel to principle, who would honor God at the loss of all things. Never would they compromise with idolaters. The king did not compel these youths to renounce their faith in favor of idolatry, but he hoped to bring this about gradually. Daily were they brought into close association with idolatrous customs and placed under the influence of the seductive rites of heathen worship so that they would renounce their religion and unite with the worship of the Babylonians. The food from the king's table was consecrated to idolatry. One partaking of it would be regarded as offering homage to the gods of Babylon. Even a mere pretense of eating the food or drinking the wine would be a denial of their faith and array them with heathenism. To Daniel, the approval of God was dearer to him than the favor of the most earthly potentate—dearer than life itself. In this resolve he was supported by his three companions.

God's promise was fulfilled to the faithful four: **"Them that honour Me, I will honour"** (1 Sam. 2:30). **"Among them all was found none like Daniel, Hananiah, Mishael, and Azariah. In all matters of wisdom and understanding, that the king enquired of them, he found them ten times better than all the magicians and astrologers that were in all his realm"** (Dan. 1:19, 20).

In physical strength and beauty, in mental vigor and literary attainment, they stood unrivalled. The erect form, the firm elastic step, the fair countenance, the undimmed senses were insignia of the nobility of those who allow God to be their teacher. Through the fidelity to the principles of temperance shown by the Hebrew youth, God is speaking to the youth of today. There is need of men who like Daniel will do and dare

Old Testament Prophets ♦ 19

for the cause of right. Pure hearts, strong hands, and fearless courage are needed. To every soul Satan comes with temptation in many alluring forms on the point of indulgence of appetite. The adversary of souls directs his temptations to the enfeebling and degrading of the physical powers. His success often means the surrender of the whole being to evil.

The life of Daniel and his fellows is a demonstration of what God will do for those who yield themselves to Him and with the whole heart seek to accomplish his purpose.

HOSEA

"Rejoice not, O Israel ... for thou hast gone a whoring from thy God ... They shall not dwell in the Lord's land; but ... shall return unto Egypt, and they shall eat unclean things ..." (Hosea 9:1–3).

Israel is portrayed as prostituting itself away from God. God used Gomer (Hosea's harlot wife), by divine command to hammer home this point. Israel never literally returned to Egyptian captivity, thus this portion of his prophecy is entirely symbolic.

God's people, regardless of their generation, are portrayed as returning unto Egypt to eat unclean foods. In Egypt God's chosen people had resorted to eating the unclean foods of the Egyptians. It also shows that in the latter days, spiritual Israel has done likewise.

Spiritual Egypt is symbolic with slavery. Why would God's children again clamor for the unclean flesh pots of Egypt when God has delivered them out of such filthy bondage?

Jesus and Disciples

Jesus sat down to dine with a Pharisee who noted that He had not washed His hands according to Jewish rituals before eating. Jesus used an object lesson to reveal what was lacking inwardly in the religious experience of these leaders:

"Now do ye Pharisees make clean the outside of the cup and the platter; but your inward part is full of ravening and wickedness. Ye fools, did not He that made that which is without make that which is within also?" (Luke 11:39).

Jesus offers a solution for outward religious actions but inward filthy hearts, and it is remarkably similar to what He told the rich young ruler: "Give alms of such things as ye have; and behold, all things are clean unto you" (Luke 11:41).

Jesus did not say if the Pharisees were to give offerings from softened hearts they would be allowed to eat unclean foods.

"Then came together unto Him the Pharisees, and certain of the scribes, which came from Jerusalem. And when they saw some of His disciples eat bread with defiled, that is to say, with unwashen, hands, they found fault.

"For the Pharisees, and all the Jews, except they wash their hands oft, eat not, holding the tradition of the elders.

"And when they come from the market, except they wash, they eat not. And many other things there be, which they have received to hold as the washing of cups, and pots, brasen vessels, and of tables. Then the Pharisees and scribes asked Him, 'Why walk not Thy disciples according to the tradition of the elders, but eat bread with unwashen hands?' He answered and said unto them, 'Well hath Esaias prophesied of you hypocrites, as it is written, This people honoureth Me with their lips, but their heart is far from Me. Howbeit in vain do they worship Me, teaching for doctrines the commandments of men. For laying aside the commandment of God, ye hold the tradition of men, as the washing of pots and cups: and many other such like things ye do.' And He said unto them, 'Full well ye reject the commandment of God, that ye may keep your own tradition'" (Mark 7: 1–9).

In this setting, Jesus then utters these famous words, "Hearken unto Me every one of you, and understand: There is nothing from without a man, that entering into him can defile him: but the things which come out of him, those are they that defile the man. If any man have ears to hear, let him hear" (Mark 7: 14–16).

Jesus' disciples were puzzled at their Master's counsel and "Asked Him concerning the parable. And He saith unto them, 'Are ye so without understanding also? Do ye not perceive that whatsoever thing from without entereth into the man, it cannot defile him; Because it entereth not into his heart, but into the belly, and goeth out into the draught, purging all meats?' And He said, 'That which cometh out of the man, that defileth the man. For from within, out of the heart of men, proceed evil thoughts, adulteries, fornications, murders. Thefts, covetousness, wickedness, deceit, lasciviousness, an evil eye, blasphemy, pride, foolishness; All these evil things come from within, and defile the man'" (Mark 7:17–23).

The Jews taught a ritual of ceremonial washing of the hands before partaking of their meal. But, there is no commandment from God in the entire Bible, which forbids eating food with unwashed, or even dirty hands. This Pharisaic tradition is in question here, not the universal food laws.

Jesus, His disciples, the Pharisees and the Scribes, were all Jews. The thought of eating an unclean meat such as pork would have never entered their minds. If the Pharisees thought Jesus was claiming their food laws were abolished, they would have immediately protested with much more vigor than expressed here. In the entire New Testament there is not one howling protest from the Jews towards Jesus, the disciples or later apostles for eating unclean meats. Did the Pharisees simply ignore a massive shift in theology proposed by Jesus? For those who strained at a gnat over matters such as washing ceremonies, it was not in their makeup to ignore any matter pertaining to traditions of the elders.

Jesus dealt with the matter for what it was—the tradition of men—and was sternly rebuked for it. Jesus pointed out the rules of the Pharisees concerning meticulous washings as being the commandments of men and called them hypocrites.

An unchanging Christ gave the plain command to Noah, and Moses regarding unclean foods. The Pharisees were following the direct commandment of God to eat clean foods and they were not rebuffed by Christ for so doing.

Many claim at this juncture Jesus purified all meats. In the original manuscript the Greek word translated *meats* is *broma*, which simply means *"that which is eaten."*

Accordingly, some Bible translators write *"purging all foods."* The basic purpose of the stomach is to purify whatever a person eats, before the waste is eliminated. This understanding reveals fanatic Pharisees for demanding cleansing ceremonies on body and utensils before eating. However, some eager translators add *"Thus He declared all foods clean."* But this phrasing is always in parentheses, which means it is a personal interpretation of the scripture, and is not in the original manuscript. If today's theologians were Christ's disciples, they would have immediately begun eating pork and other unclean foods causing an unparalleled tumult with the Jews. The original disciples never did such a thing.

Jesus came to sweep away the dead commandments of men and return them unto worshipping a living God. Away with the cruel additions of men such as the Jews forbidding healing the sick or picking corn on the Sabbath day when men were hungered.

The teaching of Jesus purifies the corrupt character in man, so that through repentance, man might have the gift of eternal life.

In Romans 6:23 Jesus makes reference to man's eternal state, which the Pharisees were in danger of losing through their legalistic rituals.

To violate the physical laws of health brings the penalty of disease, disability, pain, sickness, and sometimes death. In Jesus' lengthy discourse with the Pharisees, He is speaking of spiritual defilement not physical health. It is not a speck of dirt that enters into a man's mouth which defiles a man spiritually but the evil that comes out of his heart. Jesus is not speaking of injuring the body through bad health practices. He is teaching transgression of the Ten Commandments—evil thoughts, adulteries, fornications, murders, thefts, covetousness, blasphemy—this is what kills a man. To claim the words of Jesus were endorsing eating unclean meats is to sadly miss the mark.

"The Lord appointed other seventy also, and sent them two and two before His face into every city and place, whither He himself would come *... Eat such things as are set before you ..."* **(Luke 10: 1, 8; emphasis added).**

Jesus would follow His disciples into some of these same homes. Prior to His death are we to assume that Jewish hosts would be feeding unclean foods to their missionary guests, except for Jesus who never partook of them?

"Take no thought for your life, what ye shall eat, or what ye shall drink ... Is not the life more than meat ..." (Matt. 6:25).

The sermon on the mount is a challenge of faith, not a sermon on allowing the unclean foods into the diet.

Christ's story of the prodigal son tells of the young man who had spent his inheritance on riotous living and when destitute took on one of the meanest jobs for a Jewish lad—feeding swine. He is rescued from this lowly existence by his forgiving father (Luke 15:11–32).

Our Lord gathered up the fragments at the miracle feeding to set an example of prudence (John 6:12–13), yet He nevertheless destroyed a herd of 200 swine after devils begged to enter into them. Fittingly, the beloved physician Luke recorded this incident concerning swine under the guidance of the Holy Spirit (Luke 8:26–39).

If you were the pig farmer how would you feel if Jesus gave clearance to eat the swine after your livelihood was destroyed?

The Mennonite descendants of Reformer Meno Simon testify that every butchered pig possesses two devil's teeth marks punctured into the front left leg of each swine originating from this incident. Queried, they energetically declare, "I have seen it with mine own eyes!"

Jesus said, *"Neither cast ye your pearls before swine, lest they trample them under their feet, and turn again and rend you"* (Matt. 7:6).

No one would cast pearls or any other precious thing in front of pigs, and there is a deeper meaning in our Lord's remark. Holiness and precious things are not compatible with swine, yet Christians cast their pearls of God-given health before swine, willfully taking into their bodies this abomination. Ill health and all manner of disease eventually rend too many.

Jesus could have used the Last Supper as a clarion call to announce to future Christendom that from henceforth we will have the privilege of eating foods once forbidden as abominations. His death would allow men access to the fleshpots that had previously been referred to as the foods of devil worship. The dinner tables of Christians could now adorn with rats, buzzards, snakes and the pig. However, there was no side dish of pork at this Passover feast, only the symbolic lamb. If God had deemed denial of unclean foods as a cruel restriction, then surely He would have lifted this unusual punishment from off the back of mankind. What better forum than the Last Supper? It didn't happen.

Jesus prophesied of the time coming when the holy temple of Israel would be destroyed, and inhabited by the hated Romans, which came to pass in AD 70: *"When ye therefore shall see the abomination of desolation spoken of by Daniel the prophet, stand in the holy place ... let him understand"* (Matt. 24:15).

Once abominations of sin are clearly understood, there is only one responsible thing for a Christian to do. *"Then let them ... flee"* (Matt. 24:16).

Literal Jews fled from the Romans into the mountains to save themselves. Literal last day Christians will flee as far as the east is from the west from every known practice of Babylonian abominations. God will not wait until we are all in heaven to say—Now I will teach you My ways. He wants a people purified now, in body and in spirit.

PETER

Peter was an eye witness to this verbal exchange between Jesus and the Pharisees. He did not interpret Jesus as sanctioning eating unclean foods, as evidenced ten years later when he refused them in the vision of Acts 10.

Long after Calvary, Peter labelled the unclean creatures in the sheet as being unfit to eat. It is certain Peter was teaching his new converts the dietary laws given by God. Apostle Peter was sent forth with a message from the One who sent him. Because Peter had no message concerning a change in dietary requirements, then we must assume Christ did not send him forth with one.

JOHN THE REVELATOR

Beloved John was also a witness of Christ's discourse with the Pharisees. In writing the very last book of the Bible, John was shown in vision the fall of the Anti-Christ and he references unclean creatures as being part of spiritual Babylon's makeup. John did not think it strange that unclean foods were referenced by the angel.

"I saw another angel come down from heaven ... and he cried mightily with a strong voice, saying, Babylon the great is fallen, is fallen, and is become the habitation of devils, and the hold of every foul spirit, and a cage of every unclean and hateful bird. For all nations have drunk the wine of the wrath of her fornication ... Come out of her, My people, that ye be not partakers of her sins, and receive not her plagues" (Rev. 18: 1–4; emphasis added).

Consistent with Old Testament prophets equating sinful nations with unclean foods, the Revelation of Jesus Christ portrays spiritual Babylon as being the hold of unclean birds and warns of her plagues to follow. A call goes out from the fourth angel of Revelation to come out of Babylon's stranglehold of unclean birds and the like. In an unusually tender verse, God calls those partaking of the practices of Babylon "My People." He does not call dedicated Christians who are following false gospel and sitting at the pork barrel dirty rascals for they are called His people. God redeems His own in agape love and they are drawn unto Him.

"The Revelation of Jesus Christ ... to shew unto His servants the things which must shortly come to pass ..." (Rev. 1:1).

How odd, if Jesus Christ, the author of the Book of Revelation, would choose to use the symbolism of unclean birds to depict wickedness at the highest levels if He had washed away their forbiddance at the cross. If you believe in mixed messages that allow eating unclean meats, it will be at your peril. Perhaps the Revelation of Jesus through the prophet John can be a revelation to your soul in regard to putting away unclean meats.

For many Christians, Daniel is the greatest of all prophets. He prophesied of four nations who would rule the world in succession. The Book of Daniel is the key that unlocks understanding of its companion prophecy—The Book of Revelation. None of this would have been possible without initial victory at the tables of idolatry. Daniel remains a folk hero of the highest regard among the Jews until this day for his unwavering stand on refusing the King's diet. "Behold, there stood other two, the one on this side of the bank of the river, and the other on that side of the bank of the river" (Dan. 12:5). Some theologians have concluded the two prophets standing on opposite sides of the banks of the river were Daniel and his counterpart John. Could these prophets, joined at the hip in Scriptural harmony, be one a follower of God's dietary laws and the other an unclean meat eater?

If you believe in mixed messages that allow eating unclean meats, it will be at your peril. Perhaps the Revelation of Jesus through the prophet John can be a revelation to your soul in regard to putting away unclean meats

Revelation tells of a remnant people "Having His Father's name written in their foreheads" (Rev. 14:1).

A people who "Sung a new song before the throne ..." (Rev. 14:3).

"These are they which follow the Lamb whithersoever He goeth. These were redeemed from among men ... And in their mouths was found no guile: for they are without fault before the throne of God" (Rev. 14:3–5).

No spiritual or physical guile is found in their mouths for they are the 144,000.

NEW COVENANT

Did Jesus announce an important doctrinal change would be a part of the New Covenant? The everlasting covenant given to Abraham was the New Covenant in verity and you cannot improve upon this: **"Abram ... believed in the Lord and He counted it to him for righteousness"** (Gen. 15:6).

This New Covenant wasn't given to Abraham first, for the Bible says:

"By faith Abel ... was righteous ... and by it, he being dead yet speaketh ..." (Heb. 11:4).

"By faith Enoch was translated ... for before his translation he had this testimony, that he pleased God" (Heb. 11:5).

Without faith it is impossible to please Him" (Heb. 11:6).

"By faith Noah ... became heir of the righteousness which is by faith" (Heb. 11:7).

Some will say, how can a person experience righteousness by faith under the Old Covenant when Jesus is clearly the heartbeat of the New Covenant? Moses is in heaven because they **"Did all drink the same spiritual drink: for they drank of that spiritual Rock that followed them: and that Rock was Christ"** (1 Cor. 10:4).

Old Testament believers were saved simply by believing in the Saviour to come as illustrated through the sacrificial system. The Jews had changed the Covenant from believing in Jesus for salvation into trusting in their own works. Whenever this happens you have the Old Covenant experience going on. Righteousness by faith = New Covenant; Righteousness by works = Old Covenant. It is not time sensitive, neatly divided at Calvary; it can happen anywhere, anytime, to anyone. Partakers of the pure New

Covenant, regardless of their era, never ate unclean foods, and never will. Are we to believe there is a changed New Covenant, that Jesus brought a more powerful righteousness by faith message which adds only the unclean foods from the previous New Covenant given Abraham? One which allows meats to be eaten that were once declared by God to be abominations?

When men take it upon themselves to add to God's covenant they fulfil the words of Christ to John the Revelator: **"If any man shall add unto these things, God shall add unto him the plagues that are written in this book"** (Rev. 22:18).

At the Cross

The motto of Dwight L. Moody, famous evangelist of the late 1800s, was: *"Put me down anywhere in the Old Testament and it will lead me to the foot of the Cross."*

When sin first entered this world, a symbolic sacrifice was made by **"The Lamb slain from the foundation of the world"** (Rev. 13:8). Jesus would not die for 4,000 years but God speaking of it was equivalent to Jesus dying in the Garden of Eden.

From Adam and Eve onward all benefited from Christ's sacrifice. God spake the entire world into existence, His speaking of the Edenic sacrifice of Jesus slain was proof it had already transpired by faith. Enoch was translated right out of this world because of it, Elijah rode the chariot into heaven because of it, and Moses was resurrected because of this spoken Word.

Every sacrifice made of innocent clean animals pointed forward to Calvary. Feast days were symbols of the life and times of Jesus Christ meeting their glorious fulfillment on Golgotha, where many types were surpassed in glory by the Anti-type.

The feast days brilliantly pointed to Jesus but the complex sacrificial system of innocent animals being sacrificed was ablated when the literal Lamb of God was slain. A better day, a better Way had come. This included ending the Passover. The service of the first Passover, blood sprinkled upon every believer's doorpost, and unleavened bread eaten with bitter herbs, pointed forward to Christ, of whom the Jews still yearn for. Every believer, from Abel to Malachi **"Did all drink the same spiritual drink"** (1 Cor. 10:4).

David devotes the longest chapter in the Bible to his love for the Laws of Moses and the Ten Commandments: **"Thy statutes have been my songs in the house of my pilgrimage"** (Ps. 119:54). The priests of the Holy and Most Holy Place where God dwelt, declared, **"Thy way, O God, is in the sanctuary ..."** (Ps. 77:13).

Ordinances done away with at the cross involved the Laws of Moses, each one beautifully pointing to Christ as the sin bearer. There was nothing nailed to the cross dating pre-Moses. God's Ten Commandments remained intact as they were followed by all believers since the beginning of time.

Marriage, ordained in the Garden of Eden, also remained a sacred institution. The universal dietary laws remained unchanged from Noah's day. Nowhere and at no time or place, did unclean foods ever point forward to Christ. They remained a hated abomination to God. To surmise that Christ's death on the Cross gave credence to partake of the filth of uncleanliness is a sad error. John the Baptist cried out to behold the Lamb, not a symbolic unclean creature who would soon sanctify lizards, squirrels, mice, dogs and pigs for eating. There is no fulfillment at the cross changing unclean animals into the eating type. Men are changed at Calvary; the Bible did not say unclean creatures were. What biological change took place to transform dietary abominations into proper articles of food from a prior state of diseased sewers of filth? Did God change the organic makeup of vitamin and mineral content of unclean foods at the cross? Did God change man's physical ability to assimilate such imbalance after Calvary?

Later in this book you will marvelously see how multiple stomachs purify food. When God created man and the animal kingdom He declared the original creation to be very good. God did not seek to improvise the plan of creation 4,000 years down the road to specifically accommodate a certain class of abominable creatures for food.

In the Messianic Psalms, we catch a glimpse of Jesus hanging on the cross for a world who knew Him not, **"Thou hast made Me an abomination unto them ..."** (Ps. 88:8).

"For He hath made Him to be sin for us, who knew no sin; that we might be made the righteousness of God in Him" (2 Cor. 5:21).

In tasting death for every man, every vile and abominable sin flowed through Jesus veins as if He Himself had committed them. **"Who His own self bare our sins in His own body on the tree ..."** (1 Peter 2:24). God was destroying sin in the personage of His only begotten Son. It is flawed to reason that since Jesus became Corporate Sin, all things are now lawful for me and I am free to commit murder, adultery, theft, idolatry, covetousness, and eat abominable things. For **"We, being dead to sins, should live unto righteousness: by whose stripes we are healed"** (2 Peter 2:24).

In not one instance of the great exchange—sin for righteousness—is anything but holy living expected from the believers. If a Christian sat at the church social and dined upon snake, buzzard, squid, mice, cat, and pork, he would surely fulfill this prophecy: **"He was despised and we esteemed Him not"** (Isa. 53:3). We, who were being bitten by serpents all the day long, can look to the Cross and see our beloved Savior dying the cursed death of a serpent on a pole.

The Hebrew rendering of serpent as found in the Messianic Psalm 22 is a humbling read:

"My God, My God, why hast Thou forsaken Me? ... I am a worm and no man; a reproach of men, and despised of the people" (Ps. 22:1, 6).

Worm in the Hebrew translates out as *"serpent, snake, maggot."* Jesus died for the Corporate Sin of the world and became part of this fulfillment **"Cursed is everyone that hangeth on a tree"** (Gal. 3:13). If one from the unreached jungle asked the meaning of the gospel and a missionary replied, *"Break every Commandment, live promiscuously, and eat every rodent you can find,—all with God's blessing"*—the heathen might ask, *"What kind of gospel is the this?"* The mother of abominations rejoices when Christians eat unclean foods.

ABOLISHED AT CALVARY?

The most difficult of all arguments in favour of eating unclean foods is missed almost altogether by theologians. The dietary laws of Moses were quite intricate in nature and involved much more than a simple list of eat and don't eat certain animals. It involved touching their carcass, washing utensils, rites of purification should one become unclean, and a long list of minute details. The question needs to be addressed: Why are these additional stipulations not applicable to modern Christians today?

In their own way, each of the unclean rituals, like all other Old Testament ceremonial laws, were meant to draw a people far removed from God back to Him through His Son Jesus Christ. We do not understand the implications of many of these ceremonies and thankfully they are no longer necessary. What was good enough for Adam, Abel, Enoch, Noah, Job and Abraham is good enough for me. I know who Jesus is and what he sacrificed for my salvation. I do not need ceremonial laws surrounding the dietary laws to remind me of this fact. As a Christian, it will be an honour to eat the way Jesus ate and avoid contaminating myself with the foods He called an abomination.

"Let no man therefore judge you in meat, or in drink, or in respect of an holy day, or of the new moon, or of the Sabbath days" (Col. 2:16). Advocates of eating unclean use this text with gusto to rebuke anyone who would dare to judge them on this matter. Paul is speaking to Gentile converts who were under judgement from the Jews to retain the full package of the ceremonial laws of Moses which were nailed to the Cross. There were ceremonies for eating and drinking, the celebration for the new moon, and additional Sabbath feast days on top of the original day of rest, all of which pointed to Christ. These were no longer necessary: *"Blotting out the handwriting of ordinances ... and took it out of the way, nailing it to His cross ... which are a shadow of things to come ..."* (Col 2:14, 17).

Paul offers liberty to all including a touch not / handle not portion of the dietary law which was added by men (in addition to the command God gave to not touch the swine's flesh): *"Touch not, taste not, handle not; after the commandments and doctrines of men ..."* (Col. 2:21). *"Wherefore, if ye be dead with Christ from the rudiments of the world, why as though living in the world, are ye subject to ordinances?"* (Col. 2:20).

In our day, he that offers an animal sacrifice will be as if he had offered swine's flesh. The Saviour, having paid the supreme sacrifice once and for all is treated as if His sacrifice had been in vain. Animal sacrifices today, so right in pre-Calvary days, are so heinous to be regarded as on par with offering the worst of all abominations—swine's blood (Isa. 66:3).

CEREMONIAL LAWS NAILED TO THE CROSS

- Given to Israel in Moses' handwriting after four generations of captivity in Egypt (Exod. 20:240 and administered through Aaron's Levitical priesthood.
- Temporary sister law to the grand moral law, very complex in ceremonies, rituals, symbolism and festivals; considered to be a good law which pointed forward to Messiah (Ps. 119).
- Part of the schoolmaster to bring us unto Christ (Gal. 3:24–26), not written upon men's hearts, considered a witness against us (Deut. 31:26).
- Part of Day of Atonement, placed by the side of the Ark, involved personal loss.
- Involved judicial, civil and additional dietary, totaling 613 laws (the Jews believe 365 for solar days of the year, and 245 equaling the number of human body parts) which invoked all five senses. Was added to by the scribes and Pharisees with excruciating detail.
- Geographically limited, contained laws for rulers, the ruled, foreigners, and families including instruction on farming and clothing.
- Met a complete and utter fulfillment in Jesus at Calvary.

From the Puritan days onward, the temptation has been for men to fall back under portions of the ceremonial laws. Torah-submissive Christians believe the ceremonial laws are eternal, such as keeping the Passover and feast days.

Paul's counsel should speak plainly today to those increasing number of Christians determined to once again keep the feast days of Israel as part of their gospel. *"Why compellest thou the Gentiles to live as do the Jews?"* (Gal. 2:14).

Peter's Vision

This is by far the most popular scripture used to justify eating unclean foods. Anything other than a surface reading quickly explains God's purpose of this strange dream. The main characters in this story are the Apostle Peter, believing Jews, Cornelius the Roman soldier and his underlings, the angel sent to Cornelius, the angel sent to Peter, and the convicting power of the Holy Spirit.

"Peter went up upon the housetop to pray about the sixth hour: And he became very hungry, and would have eaten: but while they made ready, he fell into a trance, and saw heaven opened, and a certain vessel descending unto him, as it had been a great sheet knit at the four corners, and let down to the earth: Wherein were all manner of four-footed beasts of the earth, and wild beasts, and creeping things, and fowls of the air. And there came a voice to him, 'Rise, Peter; kill, and eat.' But Peter said, 'Not so Lord; for I have never eaten any thing that is common or unclean'" (Acts 10: 9–14).

Bible scholars agree Peter's vision occurred approximately ten years after Jesus' death on the cross. Peter had been present when Jesus told the Pharisees it was not what went into a man that made him unclean but what came out. Peter obviously never interpreted this to mean that new believers could eat unclean foods or he would have not questioned God's command at this time. There is no way the apostle was teaching new converts to eat unclean when he wouldn't eat it himself. Peter, like the other apostles, was slowly weaning off the ceremonial laws and feast days which had met their end. But the dietary laws of health remained steadfast in Peter's lifestyle along with the Ten Commandments.

"And the voice spake unto him again the second time, 'What God hath cleansed, that call not thou common.' This was done thrice" (Acts 10:15, 16). The Apostle Peter never got over denying his Lord three times and because of it, according to historians, he did not feel worthy to be crucified right side up (John 21:18, 19).

Yet, Peter again denies the voice of God three times when he refuses His direct command to eat unclean foods. Are we to assume that Peter was the rebellious apostle who never learned?

"And the vessel was received up again into heaven. Now while Peter doubted in himself what this vision which he had seen should mean, behold, the men which were sent from Cornelius had made inquiry for Simon's house, and stood before the gate, And called, and asked whether Simon, which was surnamed Peter, were lodged there. While Peter thought on the vision, the Spirit said unto him, 'Behold, three men seek thee. Arise therefore, and get thee down, and go with them, doubting nothing: for I have sent them.' Then Peter went down to the men which were sent unto him from Cornelius; and said, 'Behold, I am he whom ye seek: what is the cause wherefore ye are come?' And they said, 'Cornelius the centurion, a just man, and one that feareth God, and of good report among all the nation of the Jews, was warned from God by an holy angel to send for thee into his house, and to hear words of thee.' And as he talked with him, he went in, and found many that were come together" (Acts 10:17–27).

Cornelius by inspiration had sent three men to fetch Peter. Somewhere between this point and his arrival at the home of Cornelius, Peter grasped the true meaning of this vision. Cornelius had gathered together his relatives and close friends to hear the word of God through the Apostle Peter. The Apostle had no inhibitions toward entering a household full of Gentiles to preach.

"And he said unto them, 'Ye know now that it is an unlawful thing for a man that is a Jew to keep company, or come unto one of another nation; but God hath shewed me that I should not call any common or unclean'" (Acts 10:28).

Peter's vision unlocked the long-closed door of separation between Jew and Gentile. The ancient Israelites, and the Jews of Peter's day, were forbidden to associate with Gentiles (non-Israelites) because of their religious practices, which were considered abominations in the sight of God. The Jews had long been warned that association with them would eventually cause the Israelites to stumble. The Gentiles were considered unclean to the Jews. They prided themselves on being the natural descendants of Abraham, Isaac and Jacob.

Christianity was to be a holy nation, not from the seed of man, but by the spirit of God. The Jews once held exclusive rights of the gospel, but with this vision religious history changed. The gospel would now go immediately into the world without hindrance. We are Christians today in a large part thanks to this vision and to relegate its vital message as a sermon on eating a few unclean foods is to deny a pivotal turning point in Biblical understanding. The fact that most Christians cling to this vision as proof they can eat unclean foods reveals a widespread gospel problem of Christians being casual readers of text.

Peter's vision unlocked the long-closed door of separation between Jew and Gentile

There had been notable exceptions of this separation between Jew and Gentile in the past, such as Captain Naaman the Syrian who gladly received the gospel. The mixed multitude of faithful who left Egypt with Moses; a converted Babylonian, Nebuchadnezzar is the author of Daniel chapter 4. Jesus steadily ministered unto the Gentiles inviting them into the believers' fold which further incited the Pharisees against Him. The long-foreshadowed day when all believers would be equal in God's site officially arrived with this vision.

Later, at the Council of Jerusalem, Peter recounted this vision which God had brought to him. He related the plain interpretation of God's Word which was given to him almost immediately in his summons to go to the Gentile centurion and instruct him in the faith of Christ.

The same light and glory that was reflected upon the circumcised Jews, shone also upon the uncircumcised Gentiles. This was the warning of God that he should not regard the one as inferior to the other; for the blood of Jesus Christ could cleanse all from all uncleanness.

If the Apostle Paul later abolished the dietary laws as most Christians claim, then why is there not one syllable from Peter affirming this action? Why did John or James not write or talk about it? Was this Paul's burden alone? Why the Apostles' silence over such a supposed change?

Jerusalem Council AD 51

After much witnessing to the Gentiles, Paul and Barnabas were ordered to attend a Council at Jerusalem. Disputes regarding the laws of Moses had arisen amongst Jewish converts who felt the new Gentile converts should keep certain aspects.

"Certain men which came down from Judaea taught the brethren and said, *'Except ye be circumcised after the manner of Moses, ye cannot be saved.'* When therefore Paul and Barnabas had no small dissension and disputation with them, they determined that Paul and Barnabas, and certain other of them, should go up to Jerusalem unto the apostles and elders about this question" (Acts 15:1, 2). Those known to be present at the Council of Jerusalem were Paul, Barnabas, Titus, Jewish believers from Antioch and Jerusalem, as well as Peter, James, and John.

Jewish Christians were concerned about centuries of Jewish tradition being swallowed up in the onslaught of Gentile converts void of the religious history of Judaism. The dissension and disputations between Paul and the Jewish converts over circumcision was so intense it basically halted their work. These Jewish converts sent Paul and company to Jerusalem for a hastily called conference, having confidence the leaders of the Christian church would back them on keeping circumcision in the plan for Gentiles. Unlike a growing number of Christians today, bent on keeping the feast days of Israel, it appears these zealots of Judaism did not attempt to urge the adherence of feast days on the Gentiles at this council even though they were gathering in Jerusalem to keep the feast days themselves. Paul went into this meeting knowing that in Christ, type had met anti-type, thus rendering valueless the divinely appointed ceremonies and sacrifices of the Jewish religion.

Eating unclean foods and the relevance of the moral law of the Ten Commandments were not an issue in the field of Paul's labors, nor were these subjects addressed in the Council at Jerusalem.

The question of circumcision was warmly discussed in this assembly. For centuries circumcision had been the defining ceremony which set apart Jew from Gentile. There was much Jewish pride at stake in retaining this ancient rite.

Looking back, had the Jews missed the true meaning of circumcision? God had ordered their father Abraham to circumcise the children of Israel and every man under their roof as a token of His covenant with them. However, it was the child of the bondwoman, Ishmael, who was first circumcised with his father Abraham. (Gen. 17: 23–26). Immediately after God's promise that the Son of all nations would come from his barren wife Sarah, Abraham declared: **"O that Ishmael might live before thee!"** (Gen 17:18).

As Ishmael was the child of unbelief regarding God's promise of the Savior to come, Abraham was the father of unbelief. Thus, Abraham holds the distinction of being both the father of belief and unbelief. In the circumcision, a painful, bloody reminder was given to the children of Abraham of what their unbelief had cost. This is what the Jewish rite of circumcision symbolized, yet somehow it became a badge of pride for the chosen people. Fittingly the circumcised Pharisees became the epitome of unbelief.

When Jesus was murdered on the cross in a bloody mess, the history of spiritual circumcision drew to its painful close. Every believer in the promised Son who came from the spiritual seed of Abraham would have no further need of this identity. The Jews mistakenly upheld circumcision as a sign of their special identity as God's chosen people. They should have been thrilled to discard this sign of unbelief, instead they passionately defended the rite as necessary.

This is not to argue the widely agreed upon medical benefits of circumcision in the world today. This council only discussed circumcision as an outward spiritual sign identifying a holy people.

Peter eloquently reasoned that the Holy Ghost had descended with equal power upon both circumcised Jew and uncircumcised Gentile. He recounted the vision in which God had presented all manner of unclean beasts in the sheet with an order to eat them. Peter recounted God's words, **"What God hath cleansed, that call not thou common"** (Acts 10:15). This message proved God was no respecter of persons—He accepted and acknowledged those who feared Him and worked righteousness. This was the warning of God that men should not regard one as inferior to another, for the blood of Christ could cleanse from all uncleanness. Peter passionately asked the assembly, **"Why tempt ye God to put a yoke upon the neck of the disciples, which neither our fathers nor we were able to bear?"** (Acts 15:10).

The Council of Jerusalem simplified matters greatly for new believers where it was proclaimed they should not eat foods containing blood. And this is where we are at today as Christians.

A type of Melchisadek now resided in heaven as our High Priest, saying, **"Take My yoke upon you, and learn of Me; for I am meek and lowly in heart: and ye shall find rest for your souls. For My yoke is easy, and My burden light"** (Matt. 11: 28–30).

The centuries-old yoke of regulations, never necessary in the pre-flood, nor in the pre-Egyptian captivity days, was finally over.

"Then all the multitude kept silence, and gave audience to Barnabas and Paul, declaring what miracles and wonders God had wrought among the Gentiles by them" (Acts 15:12).

James was the clear leader of the early church, and he who presided at this council made the decision regarding circumcision: **"Wherefore my sentence is, that we trouble not them which from among the Gentiles are turned to God"** (Acts 15:19).

This council would have been the perfect New Testament opportunity for James to tell all that God had also liberalized Christians, both Jew and Gentile, to eat unclean foods and that Peter had fallen short in his understanding of his vision. He could have mentioned that Jesus had cleared the way by saying nothing that enters a man is unclean. It would have been the big news at the Council. Instead, James focused on other matters pertaining to diet. These decisions had been settled by the Holy Ghost, upon which depended the prosperity, and even the existence of the Christian church.

Among the stipulations that James said must be kept dating from Moses was: **"That ye abstain from meats offered to idols …"** (Acts 15:29).

Outside the Jewish world was a land teeming with idols and the worship of them. The book of Acts is a steady parade of conflicts between idol worshippers and Christians. After Jesus' death this was the major conflict reported in the New Testament.

Another dietary restriction came forth: **"That ye abstain from ... blood ..."** (Acts 15:29). This involved the Jewish practice of severing the animal's trachea and esophagus, the carotid artery and jugular vein with a sharp knife that had been thoroughly checked for imperfections beforehand. As much blood as possible must be removed from the meat either by soaking, salting and rinsing or by broiling over a fire.

The Gentiles practiced catching the blood which flowed from the victim of the sacrifice, and drinking it, or using it in the preparation of their food. Therefore, as things then stood, if a Jew and Gentile came to eat at the same table, the former would be shocked and outraged by the habits and manners of the latter.

A final dietary restriction involved the strangling of animals was given by James: **"That ye abstain from ... things strangled"** (Acts 15:29). This also pertained in part to not draining the blood properly.

One other stipulation was brought forth: **"That they abstain from ... fornication"** (Acts 15:29). The Gentiles, especially the Greeks, were extremely licentious and in accepting Christianity, had united the truth to their unsanctified natures while continuing to practice fornication. The Jewish Christians could not tolerate such immorality, which was not even regarded as criminal by the Greeks.

The Jews held it proper that circumcision and ceremonial laws should be brought to the Gentiles as a test of their sincerity and devotion. But it was not to be so.

THE GENTILES WOULD NOT BE ASKED TO FOLLOW:

(1) Ceremonial laws containing animal sacrifices.
(2) Feast days including the Passover.
(3) Additional holy days outside of the fourth commandment Sabbath day.
(5) Rites of purification.
(6) Man-made vows to God.
(7) The earthly Levitical priesthood and all it entailed.
(8) Thousands of man-made regulations kept by the descendants of the Levitical priesthood.

Liberty would reign. This good news was not accepted unanimously by Jewish believers. Paul was looked upon by conservative Jews as a rebel threatening the history of Judaism through his radical teachings of Christ. Both non-believing Jews and legalistic believing Jews fought Paul on these matters, not resting until they finally put him in his grave.

Undaunted, the Apostle Paul went forth armed with a mandate to uphold the church of Christ with very few regulations to discourage new converts by. The matter pertaining to eating foods sacrificed to idols, was a delicate issue percolating in Corinth, a common practice that would need to be addressed upon his return.

How much power and influence did centuries of Jewish tradition bear upon the Christian church? On Paul's final trip to Jerusalem (which would result in his eventual beheading in Rome) he met with James and the elders of the Christian church. Paul **"declared particularly what things God had wrought among the Gentiles by his ministry. And when they heard it, they glorified the Lord"** (Acts 21:19, 20).

James clearly indicates there were two gospels in operation, one for Jews and one for Gentiles: **"As touching the Gentiles which believe, we have written and concluded that they observe no such thing, save only that they keep themselves from things offered to idols, and from blood, and from strangled, and from fornication"** (Acts 21:25).

Then James said unto Paul: **"Thou seest brother, how many thousands of Jews there are which believe; and they are all zealous of the law: And they are informed of thee, that thou teachest all the Jews which are among the Gentiles to forsake Moses, saying that they ought not to circumcise their children, neither walk after the customs. What is it therefore? The multitude must needs come together: for they will hear that thou art come. Do therefore this that we say to thee: We have four men which have a vow on them; Them take, and purify thyself with them, and be at charges with them, that they may shave their heads: and all may know that those things, whereof they were informed concerning thee, are nothing; but that thou thyself also walkest orderly, and keepest the law"** (Acts 21: 19–24).

This shameful command from James and his elders came to the weary Apostle who had faithfully brought to the original council, Titus, an uncircumcised Greek (Gal. 2:3). However, after the Council of Jerusalem, Paul urged Timothy, he of a Jewish mother, to be circumcised so as not to outrage the Jews (Acts 16:3). Thus Paul, who had bowed to Jewish pressures regarding the circumcision, obediently followed the misguided council of James. He was seized by the irate Jews anyway and shipped off to Rome where he would spend his final days in captivity.

We can only speculate whether James repented of his weakness when he was martyred by the same fanatical Jews shortly afterward, proof that a legalist can never be satisfied by compromise.

What the apostles seemingly could not do—shake off 2,000 years of Jewish ceremonial laws—it is the responsibility of every Christian to do. The temptation for the modern Christian is found in the beauty and intrinsic detail of these laws, and why not? God ordained them, David called them a delight, and they served an excellent purpose. But in Christ all of the ceremonial laws came to a fulfillment. To re-enact these laws is to revert to Judaism and bondage.

Idol Worship

Most of the proof texts given by Christians to sanction the use of unclean foods revolve around Apostle Paul's teaching directed at new Christians to stop eating foods sacrificed to idols. It is a subject of little relevance to modern Christians in North America and Europe. To approach the subject of Paul's writings objectively we must examine the context in which his words were written. To do so is to understand the prevalence of idol worship in the world leading up to New Testament Corinth where the subject finally came to a head.

"Learn not the way of the heathen … for the customs of the people are vain … They are upright as the palm tree, but speak not: they must needs be borne, because they cannot go. Be not afraid of them; for they cannot do evil, neither also is it in them to do good. Forasmuch as there is none like unto Thee O Lord; Thou art great, and Thy name is great in might … Thus shall ye say unto them, 'The gods that have not made the heavens and the earth, even they shall perish from the earth, and from under these heavens'" (Jer. 10:2–11).

ANTEDILUVIAN TIMES

This period from Adam to Noah ushered in the destruction of the world because the people's every thought was utter wickedness. One thing we learned from Cain's offering is that all forms of creature worship involve a sacrifice and many involved foods. Those like faithful Enoch in the Antediluvian world were rare. If these generations were not serving God, then in the words of Bob Dylan (during a brief span when he embraced Christianity) *"You've got to serve somebody."* It is safe to assume that idol worship was a dominant force during the first centuries after Adam. **"Fear the Lord … put away the gods which our fathers served on the other side of the flood …"** (Josh. 24:13, 14).

EGYPTIAN IDOLS

"At the beginning there was naught save darkness and water. The spirit of the night was the Great Mother, APET, and her first born was AH, the moon child."

PTAH

Great Father, first born of all gods, worshipped as the male earth spirit.

HATHOR

The sky goddess of turquoise.

RA

The sun god.

AMON-RA

Bearded man with lunar and solar symbols.

SET

Egyptian god of chaos who embodied the principle of hostility, if not outright evil. An adversary of the good gods, this god had a cult following in Egypt.

OSIRIS

Was the human incarnation, god of the dead and underworld.

ISIS

Goddess of healing.

NUT

The sky and water goddess.
NEITH
The earth goddess who symbolized growth.
NEHEB-KAU
The serpent goddess represented by a flying serpent with a human head, arms and legs, with an interest in the souls of the dead.

Not only was idol worship entrenched in Egypt, but the populace was also steeped in creature worship. The fish was sacred in Egypt, as were the bull, goose, frog, doves and pigeons. The hare was identified with a god of the underworld. The crocodile held superstitious regard. Animals were capable of being gods or devils depending upon which spirit possessed them. Dogs and cats were viewed spiritually as was the lion and the hippopotamus. There was a corn god. Basically, if there was a creature residing in Egypt it possessed some form of spiritual value.

After centuries of captivity in Egypt, idol worship among the Jews had descended to new lows. So serious was idol worship that the first two of the Ten Commandments dealt with Egyptian idol worship and every form of idol worship henceforth.

"I am the Lord thy God, which have brought thee out of the land of Egypt, out of the house of bondage. Thou shalt have no other gods before Me. Thou shalt not make unto thee any graven image, or any likeness of any thing that is in heaven above, or that is in the earth beneath, or above, or that is in the earth beneath, or that is in the water under the earth. Thou shalt not bow down thyself to them, nor serve them" (Exod. 20:1–4).

God desired a clean start for His chosen people after what they had been subject to all the days of their lives in Egypt. These commandments counteracted a false gospel through idol worship brought forth by Satan who knew the coming Christ child was looming on the horizon. The Egyptian idols were depicted as being involved in a constant war between good and evil.

The Jewish nation was delivered from Egyptian captivity by the miraculous parting of the Red Sea and immediately received the written command of God concerning idol worship. The freed slaves responded by delving into idol worship when they felt God had removed Moses as their leader during his prolonged absence while upon the mountain.

"The people gathered themselves unto Aaron, and said unto him, 'Up, make us gods, which shall go before us' … and all the people brake off the golden earrings which were in their ears, and brought them to Aaron. And he received them at their hand, and fashioned it with a graving tool, after he had made it a molten calf; and they said, 'These be thy gods O

Israel, which brought thee up out of the land of Egypt.' And when Aaron saw it, he built an altar before it; and Aaron made a proclamation, and said, 'Tomorrow is a feast unto the Lord.' And they rose up early on the morrow, and offered burnt offerings, and brought peace offerings; and the people sat down to eat and to drink, and rose up to play"** (Exod. 32:1–6).

From this account it is clear the Jews believed God would bless their idol worship. They attributed their deliverance out of Egypt to these gods. Their god of choice was the sacred calf of Egypt. Every form of idol worship involved a feast in honor of the gods. Part of their punishment from God mocked their eating sacrifices to these false gods:

> *The North American mind cannot begin to fathom the scope of idol worship with which the Apostles met*

"Moses ... took the calf which they had made, and burned it in the fire, and ground it to powder, and strawed it upon the water, and made the children of Israel drink of it" (Exod. 32:20).

There was further punishment as the next day the Levites drew their swords and "there fell of the people that day about three thousand men" (Exod. 32:28). Regarding idol worship, "Moses said unto the people, 'Ye have sinned a great sin ...'" (Exod. 32:30).

Decades later, Joshua is still preaching to Israel about worshipping the false gods of Egypt: "I have given you a land ... now therefore fear the Lord ... put away the gods which your fathers served in Egypt" (Josh. 24:13, 14).

And so it was from the beginning—idol worship, sacrifices to idols, eating foods sacrificed to idols—which God decreed against in the Ten Commandments, calling it a grievous sin.

NEW TESTAMENT IDOLS

The North American mind cannot begin to fathom the scope of idol worship with which the Apostles met. This was Satan's trump card for the age, for every idol also paralleled the Hebrew gospel in some manner. Some of the better-known gods of worship during New Testament times were:

APRHRODITE

Greek goddess of love.

"For God so loved the world, that He gave His only begotten Son, that whosoever believeth in Him should not perish, but have everlasting life" (John 3:16).

Idol Worship ◆ 47

APOLLO

Greek and Roman god of prophecy, healing, and arts whose ruined temples, theatre and statue remain a major tourist attraction.

"No prophecy of the scripture is of any private interpretation. For the prophecy came not in the old time by the will of man: but holy men of God spake as they were moved by the Holy Ghost" (2 Pet. 1:20–21).

ARES

Greek god of war.

"Pharaoh's chariots and his host hath He cast into the sea: The Lord is a man of war: the Lord is His name" (Exod. 15:3, 4).

ARTEMIS

Major Greek Olympian goddess of hunting.

"Nimrod ... began to be a mighty hunter [murderer in sin—*Strong's*] ... and the beginning of his kingdom was Babel ..." (Gen. 10:8–10).

ASCLEPIUS

Greek god of healing.

"And the people followed [Jesus] and He ... healed them that had need of healing" (Luke 9:11).

ATHENA

Greek goddess of war and wisdom whose worship became the official cult of Athens and whom the elaborate Parthenon was built including a forty-foot gold and ivory statue of her.

"There is no wisdom, nor understanding, nor counsel against the Lord" (Prov. 21:30).

ATLAS

Greek god who guarded the pillars of heaven and eventually held up the entire earth and sky.

"O Lord God of hosts, Who is a strong Lord like unto Thee? The heavens are Thine ... Thou hast a mighty arm: strong is Thy right hand, and high is Thy right hand" (Ps. 89:8, 11, 13).

CUPID

Roman god of love and Eros, his Greek counterpart.

"And we have known and believed the love that God hath to us. God is love [agape]; and he that dwelleth in love dwelleth in God, and God in him ... We love Him because He first loved us" (1 John 4:16, 19).

DEMETER

Greek goddess of plants.

"And God said, Let the earth bring forth grass, the herb yielding seed, and the fruit tree yielding fruit after his kind, whose seed is in itself upon the earth, and it was so" (Gen. 1:11).

DIANA

Greek goddess, protector of women. Temple in Ephesus was one of seven wonders of the ancient world, longer than a football field with twenty-seven columns fifty-feet high. Silver models of this temple and Diana were sold.

"A silversmith, which made silver shrines for Diana ... called together with the workman of like occupation ... and said ... Paul hath persuaded and turned away much people, saying that they be no gods which are made with hands ... that the temple of the great goddess Diana should be despised, and her magnificence should be destroyed, whom all Asia and the world worshippeth ... all with one voice about the space of two hours cried out, Great is Diana ... and of the image that fell down from Jupiter" (Acts 19:24–35).

DIONYSUS

Greek god of wine.

"Wine is a mocker, strong drink is raging: and whosoever is deceived thereby is not wise" (Prov. 20:1).

FLORA

Roman goddess of the spring and flowers.

"Blessed be the name of God for ever and ever: for wisdom and might are His: And He changeth the times and the seasons" (Dan. 2:20, 21).

HELIOS

The Greek sun god.

"And on the seventh day, God ended His work which He had made; and He rested on the seventh day ... and God blessed the seventh day and sanctified it ..." (Gen. 2:2, 3).

HEPHAESTOS

Greek god of craftsmen.

"The gold for things of gold, and the silver for things of silver, and for all manner of work to be made by the hands of artificers. And who then is willing to consecrate his service this day unto the Lord" (1 Chron. 29:5).

HERA

Greek—queen of marriage and birth.

Roman—Juno (June) protector of women.

"Master, this woman was taken in adultery, Now Moses commanded us, that such should be stoned: but what sayest Thou?" He ... said unto them, "He that is without sin among you, let him first cast a stone at her." But the woman, He said unto her, "Woman, where are those thine accusers?" She said, "No man, Lord." And Jesus said unto her, "Neither do I condemn thee: go, and sin no more" (John 8:3–11).

Idol Worship ◆ 49

HERMES
Greek god of merchants, literature, and messenger of the gods.
"And there are also many other things which Jesus did, the which, if they should be written every one, I suppose that even the world itself could not contain the books that should be written" (John 21:25).

HESTIA
Greek goddess of the home, family and hearth flame.
"Because thou hast made the Lord ... thy habitation; there shall no evil befall thee, neither shall any plague come nigh thy dwelling" (Ps. 91:9, 10).

HYPNOS
Greek god of sleep and dreams.
"There is a God in heaven that revealeth secrets ... thy dream, and the visions of thy head upon thy bed, are these ..." (Dan. 2:28).

IRIS
Greek goddess of the rainbow, the bridge from earth to heaven.
"Behold, a ladder set up on the earth, and the top of it reached to heaven: and behold the angels of God ascending and descending upon it" (Gen. 28:12).

JANUS
Roman god of new doorways, with twin faces pointing opposite (January).
"Behold, I stand at the door, and knock: if any man hear My voice, and open the door, I will come in to him and will sup with him, and he with Me" (Rev. 3:20).

JUPITER
Supreme god of the Roman Pantheon thought to cause rain and thunder.
"O God ... the clouds poured out water ... the voice of Thy thunder was in the heaven: the lightening lightened the world: the earth trembled and shook" (Ps. 77:16–18).

Mars
Roman god of agriculture (March), also the fierce red god of war.
"While the earth remained, seed time and harvest, and cold and heat, and summer and winter, and day and night shall not cease" (Gen. 8:22).

MERCURY
Roman god of commerce and good luck, who ended up on the US coin.
"Honour the Lord with thy substance, and with the first fruits of all thine increase: so shall thy barns be filled with plenty ..." (Prov. 3:9, 10).

MINERVA
Roman goddess of arts, crafts and trade.
"Sing unto the Lord, all the earth ... declare His glory among the heathen; His marvellous works among the nations" (1 Chron. 16:23, 24).

MITHRAS
Roman god of sun and truth whose rituals involved:
(1) miraculous birth of a baby
(2) baptism
(3) a sacred meal of bread and wine
(4) the promise of resurrection

(1) "The Holy Ghost shall come upon thee ... therefore also that holy thing which shall be born of thee shall be called the Son of God" (Luke 1:35).

(2) "John answered, 'There standeth one among you, whom ye know not ... Behold the Lamb of God, which taketh away the sin of the world'" (John 1:26–29).

(3) "Jesus took bread ... and said, 'Take, eat; this is My body. And He took the cup ... saying Drink ye all of it; for this is my blood ...'" (Matt. 26:26–28).

(4) Jesus said ... 'I am the resurrection, and the life ...'" (John 11:25).

NEMESIS
Greek goddess with the power to punish.
"The Lord knoweth how to ... reserve the unjust unto the day of judgement to be punished" (2 Pet. 2:9).

NEPTUNE
Roman god of the sea.
"There came down a storm of wind upon the lake and they were ... in jeopardy ... Then He arose, and rebuked the wind and the raging of the water; and they ceased and there was calm" (Luke 8:23, 24).

NIKE
Greek winged goddess of victory.
"But thanks be to God, which giveth us the victory through our Lord Jesus Christ" (1 Cor. 15:57).

OCEANUS
Greek god who ruled the oceans.
"Then the Lord answered ...Who shut up the sea with doors when it brake forth ... and said, 'Hitherto shalt thou come, but no further: and here shall thy proud waves be stayed?'" (Job 38:8, 11).

PAN

Greek god of shepherds.

"The Lord is my shepherd; I shall not want. He maketh me to lie down in green pastures; He leadeth me beside the still waters" (Ps. 23:1, 2).

PHOEBE

Greek goddess of the full moon, protector of the sanctuary.

"I consider Thy heavens, the work of Thy fingers, the moon and the stars, which Thou has ordained ... Thy way O God is in the sanctuary" (Ps. 77:13).

PLUTO

Roman god of the underworld and death, minerals of the earth, counterpart of the Greek Hades.

"Fear not them which kill the body, but are not able to kill the soul: but rather fear Him which is able to destroy both soul and body in hell" (Matt. 10:28).

POSEIDON

Principal Greek god of the seas.

"Where is the Lord God? And when he also had smitten the waters, they parted hither and thither: and Elisha went over" (2 Kings 2:14).

PROMETHEUS

Greek god who created humanity out of the clay of the ground.

"Thine hands have made me and fashioned me together ... Remember ... Thou hast made me as the clay ..." (Job 10:8, 9).

SATURN

Roman god overseeing their crops.

"Thrust in thy sickle and reap; for the time is come for thee to reap; for the harvest of the earth is ripe. And He that sat on the cloud thrust in His sickle on the earth; and the earth was reaped" (Rev. 14:15, 16).

URANUS

Greek god who manifested himself as the sky as seen on this postage stamp.

"And God made the firmament ... and called the firmament Heaven" (Gen. 1:7, 8).

VENUS

Roman goddess of love.

"When we were yet without strength, in due time Christ died for the ungodly ... God commendeth His love toward us, in that, while we were yet sinners, Christ died for us ... when we were enemies, we reconciled to God by the death of his Son" (Rom. 5: 6–10).

VESTA

Roman goddess of the hearth, widely worshipped in homes.

"The house of the righteous shall stand" (Prov. 12:7).

ZEUS

Supreme ruler of the Greek gods known for justice, law and morality, in whose honour the Olympics were held with many sacrifices to the gods.

"I beheld … the Ancient of days did sit, whose garment was white as snow, and the hair of His head like the pure wool; His throne was like the fiery flame, and His wheels as burning fire. A fiery stream issued and came forth from before Him: thousand thousands ministered unto Him, and ten thousand times ten thousand stood before Him …" (Dan. 7:9, 10).

PAGAN LITERATURE

Add to these pagan gods and goddesses centuries of influences from the greatest writers and philosophers the world has ever known, whose influence continue to shape modern society at all levels.

HOMER

The iconic Greek poet of 8th century.

PLATO

The highly influential Greek philosopher and scholar (427 BC).

HERODOTUS

The Greek father of history (485–425 BC).

ARISTOTLE

The unrivalled scholar of the ancient world (384–322 BC) with enormous pagan impact.

VIRGIL
Literary figure (70 BC) who believed the Romans possessed a superior destiny.

PAGAN FOLKLORE

Gentile history was steeped with folklore and legends bearing the intimate fabric of their many heroes whose fascinating stories were retold without end. In comparison, Biblical accounts often seemed like a tame regurgitating of legends which the pagans had heard before.

ACHILLES
Half-man, half-god who was dipped into the river by the heel and later died with a wound to the heel.

"Thou shalt bruise His heel" (Gen 3:15).

ADONIS
The beautiful youth whose shed blood turned the sea red.

"He lifted up the rod and smote the waters that were in the river ... and all the waters that were in the river turned to blood" (Exod. 7:20).

AEGEUS
King of Athens who lived in the age of a Greek prophecy foretelling a coming hero. He died grief stricken for his people.

"This is He of whom I said, After me cometh a man which is preferred before me ... that He should be made manifest to Israel ..." [John the Baptist about Jesus] (John 1:31).

HELEN
The beautiful Queen of Troy.

"Esther ... the maid was fair and beautiful ... and the king ... set the royal crown upon her head and made her queen ..." (Esther 2:7, 17).

HERACLES
Roman Hercules, the most famous of all Greek heroes and legendary strongman.

> *Gentile history was steeped with folklore and legends bearing the intimate fabric of their many heroes whose fascinating stories were retold without end. In comparison, Biblical accounts often seemed like a tame regurgitating of legends which the pagans had heard before*

"And Samson said, 'With the jawbone of an ass ... have I slain a thousand men'" (Judges 15:16).

PANDORA

The first woman formed out of clay who opened a box releasing evil spirits upon the earth, along with Hope to succour mankind.

"For in that He Himself hath suffered being tempted, He is able to succour them that are tempted" (Heb. 2:18).

ROMULUS

Founder of Rome, believed to be translated.

"By faith Enoch was translated that he should not see death ..." (Heb. 11:5).

APOSTLES FIGHT IDOLATRY

Into this myriad of philosophy, learning, and centuries of steeped pagan tradition, waded Paul and the rest of the apostles with the aim of converting their hearers to Christianity. The early strategy of the Apostles was to fight fire with fire, quoting Greek icons and poets, trying to win them over through association. This tactic was soon abandoned when it was realized only the Cross of Christ had the power to win over idolized souls. Christianity met with ferocious opposition as found in the book of Acts. Paul devotes the equivalent of three entire chapters of his writings alone to the vital subject of foods being sacrificed to idol gods.

In AD 45, Paul and Barnabas ... "Fled into ... cities of Lyconia ... and there they preached the gospel. And there sat a certain man at Lystra, impotent in his feet, being a cripple from his mother's womb, who had never walked: The same heard Paul speak: who steadfastly beholding him, and perceiving that he had faith to be healed, said with a loud voice, 'Stand upright on thy feet.' And he leaped and walked. And when the people saw what Paul had done, they lifted up their voices, saying in the speech of Lycaonia, 'The gods are come down to us in the likeness of men.' And they called Barnabas—*Jupiter*; and Paul—*Mercurius*, because he was the chief speaker. Then the priest of *Jupiter*, which was before their city, brought oxen and garlands unto the gates, and would have done sacrifice with the people. Which when the apostles ... heard of, they rent their clothes, and ran in among the people crying out, and saying, 'Sirs, why do ye these things? We also are men of like passions with you, and preach unto you that ye should turn from these vanities unto the living god, which made heaven, and earth, and the sea, and all things that are therein'" (Acts 14: 6–15; emphasis added).

Upon witnessing a miracle, the Greeks were quick to bring out a food sacrifice to offer to what they perceived as being the great heathen deities, Jupiter and Mercury come down from heaven. This belief was in harmony with their traditions that their gods visited the earth. They believed Paul to be Mercury for he was active, earnest, quick, and eloquent. Barnabas was believed to be Jupiter, the father of gods, because of his venerable appearance, his dignified bearing, and the benevolence expressed in his countenance.

The people listened to Paul who denied they were gods, with manifest impatience. Only after much persuasion, they reluctantly acknowledged their error and led the sacrificial beasts away in great disappointment. Sacrificing to Mercury and Jupiter come down from heaven would have strengthened their religion in the estimation of the world.

Opposing Jews from Antioch, bitter enemies, seized upon this opportunity convincing the rabble that this had been the miraculous work of devils who Paul and Barnabas served. The worm turned so that the heathens now considered them worse than murderers and to kill them would be doing a service to mankind. *"And having stoned Paul, drew him out of the city, supposing he had been dead"* (Acts 14:19).

"While Paul waited for them at Athens, his spirit was stirred in him, when he saw the city wholly given to idols" (Acts 17:16). The philosophers of Athens said of Paul, *"He seemeth to be a setter forth of strange gods …"* (Acts 17:18).

As Paul stood on Mars hill overlooking a congregation deeply immersed in idol worship, he saw Satan's counterfeit of the gospel story in the eyes of his hearers. There was *Prometheus,* who molded humanity out of clay; *Demeter* and *Flora,* of nature; *Athena,* all wisdom; *Atlas,* god of strength; *Aphrodite* and *Venus,* goddesses of love; *Ares,* god of war; *Apollo* the prophet; *Hypnos,* god of dreams; *Iris,* the bridge between heaven and earth; *Helios,* the sun god; *Phoebe,* protector of the sanctuary; *Pluto* and *Hades,* gods of death; *Mithras,* the miraculous baby birth, baptism, communion and the resurrection; *Asclepias,* the healer; *Pan,* god of the shepherds; and finally *Zeus,* god of gods, sitting on his throne in heaven.

Mars' Hill was one of the most sacred spots in all Athens. It was in this place that matters connected with religion were often carefully considered by men who acted as final judges on all the more important moral questions. Around Paul gathered poets, artists, and philosophers—the scholars and sages of Athens. Paul reasoned with the Greeks in language they could relate to. He showed himself familiar with their works of art, their literature, and their religion.

"For as I passed by, and beheld your devotions, I found an altar with this inscription, TO THE UNKNOWN GOD, Whom therefore ye ignorantly worship, Him declare I unto you ... Forasmuch then as we are the offspring of God, we ought not to think that the Godhead is like unto gold, or silver, or stone, graven by art and man's device. And the times of this ignorance God winked at; but now commandeth all men every where to repent ... He will judge the world in righteousness by that man whom He hath ordained; whereof He hath given assurance unto all men, in that He hath raised Him from the dead" (Acts 17:23–31).

Their opposition was predictable: "When they heard of the resurrection of the dead, some mocked: and other said, *We will hear thee again of this matter.* Howbeit certain men clave unto him and believed" (Acts 17: 32, 33).

Although the sermon at Mars' Hill was a great success, Paul was not entirely pleased with the results when he had addressed such an influential crowd of listeners. This was the last recorded time he would fight philosophy with philosophy. Paul deduced that there was only one gospel that could reach such hardened hearts.

"The Greeks seek after wisdom. But we preach Christ crucified ... unto the Greeks foolishness. But unto them which are called ... Christ the power of God, and the wisdom of God. Because the foolishness of God is wiser than men ..." (1 Cor. 1:22–24).

There was no ancient god who ever sacrificed his life for the ungodly. There were no deities who loved their enemies and died to save sinners. This concept was unthinkable and moved all who heard—some to everlasting life—and some who desired to kill the Apostle for preaching it.

Ephesus was famed for the worship of the goddess Diana and the practice of magic. The great temple of Diana was one of the wonders of the ancient world. Its magnificence made it the pride, not only of the city, but of the nation. Kings and princes had enriched it by donations while Ephesians added to its splendor as the treasure-house for the wealth of Western Asia. The idol enshrined in the sumptuous edifice was a rude, uncouth image, declared by tradition to have fallen from the sky. Upon it were inscribed mystic characters and symbols, believed to possess great power. When pronounced, they were said to accomplish wonders. When written, they were treasured as a potent charm to guard their possessor from robbers, from disease, and even from death. Costly books were written by the Ephesians to explain the meaning and use of these symbols.

May was devoted to the worship of the goddess of Ephesus attracting an immense concourse of people from all over Asia. Throughout the month, festivities were conducted with utmost pomp and splendor. The gods were represented by people chosen for this purpose, and they were worshipped. Sacrifices made to the gods, musical contests, feats of athletes, and the fierce combats between men and beasts drew admiring crowds to the vast theatres. The whole city was a scene of brilliant display and wild revelry. The air rung with sounds of joy. The people gave themselves up to feasting, drunkenness, and the vilest debauchery. This gala season was a trying occasion to believers new to the faith.

Diana

Into this scene came Paul boldly preaching the cross of Christ. It was here that God chose to work miracles of healing and casting out of demons which made a deep impression upon idolaters. There was a perceptible falling off in attendance at the national festival and in the enthusiasm of the worshippers. Many lost all confidence in the heathen gods. By the labors of Paul at Ephesus, heathen worship received a telling blow. Centuries of heathen signs and symbols were replaced by a secret new one that signified a new way of living.

Apostle Paul and Idol Foods

The city of Corinth was one of the most influential commercial centres in the world, wealthy not only in finance but in learning and elegance. The city's greatest asset was its geography, favourably situated for trade by land on its renowned roadbed or by sea. It was here that Alexander the Great was chosen to lead the Greeks against the Persians. Corinth was also renowned for its immorality and vice, particularly in the temple of Aphrodite which housed 1,000 sacred prostitutes.

Apostle Paul lived in Corinth for eighteen months and met Aquila and Priscilla there while he was employed as a self-supporting tent maker. Emperor Nero visited the city and set in motion the building a valuable canal.

With a current population of 30,000, Corinth sits forty-eight miles west of Athens on a narrow peninsula, an important link between northern and southern Greece. It remains a thriving centre for both inquisitive tourists and religious pilgrims.

Systematic excavations continue and are exhibited in the on-site Archaeological Museum of Ancient Corinth.

Most of the surviving ruins are from when the Romans rebuilt the city including the platform where Paul pled his case before the Roman governor Gallio. The temple of Apollo, which was vibrant during Paul's day, remains partially intact.

THE CORINTHIAN PROBLEM

Upon Apostle Paul's arrival, the Corinthians were not asking, *Can we eat idol food*? but *Why can't we eat idol food*? It is understandable why a dispute arose.

The Christian problem of eating food dedicated to an idol was not easily solved. Converts who turned from the worship of many sundry gods were unclear where to draw the line, or if it was even necessary to draw the line when it came to food that had been sacrificed to idols. Corinthian converts came from quite a different cultural heritage and they downplayed any dinner party held in a pagan temple which they believed had no spiritual effect on them. Paul's work was cut out to convince them otherwise. It explains why his argument begins by trying to find common ground with their perspective and it is seemingly so roundabout. Paul's expectations demanded of converts something that no other religion except Judaism required – avoiding anything that might hint that Christians sanctioned idolatry. Failure to repudiate all idolatrous associations, Paul maintains, would have dire spiritual consequences.

ANTI-SOCIAL BEHAVIOR

Occasions for eating in connection with an idol or on the premises of an idol's temple were numerous. The celebrations of many cults were closely bound up with civic and social life since religion and politics were indivisible in ancient Hellenistic city life. If Christians took part in civic life, they were expected to participate in sacrificial meals in some form of another. Those who shared the same trades (Acts 19:24–25), or a desire to worship specific gods, banded together in voluntary associations, clubs, and guilds.

Individuals might receive invitations to a banquet at a temple to celebrate, for example, a god's birthday. Sacrificial meals to various deities served as markers of class divisions on a number of different levels. The chief reason for their participation would have been the intense social pressure from their surrounding culture. Prominent Corinthian Christians would have been reluctant to shun gatherings that lubricated social relations.

Meals were viewed as opportunities to converse and build friendships as well as to further economic ties. To ignore these feasts would make Christians conspicuous outcasts

Meals were viewed as opportunities to converse and build friendships as well as to further economic ties. To ignore these feasts would make Christians conspicuous outcasts who held outlandish, anti-social, and perverse religious beliefs. Family and friends would be dismayed at their sudden change in religious practices. The pressure on Christians to conform culturally was enormous. The Corinthians did not want to draw hard and fast lines that would alienate such important persons from their lives and exclude them from society. To go the whole way, to turn from idols to serve the living God, was an act that entailed a profound re-socialization, a change of identity and primary allegiance. This was a change not many in Corinth were willing to make. The Corinthians tried desperately to balance their identity as Christians along with their assimilation to the highly competitive, pagan Corinthian culture without inviting ostracism from unbelievers which might lead to shame and material loss.

The Corinthians did not exercise theological bravado, or spiritual liberty by deliberately eating what had been offered to idols. They quite naturally did not want to give up their family and social connections.

Paul responds to the Corinthians' resistance being fully aware of the intense pressure of social norms. He wisely counsels the Corinthians that of course they can dine with friends. Paul believes the church and faith could correlate well with a life-style which remained fully integrated within Corinthian society. Or as Jesus put it, "I pray not that thou shouldest take them out of the world, but that thou shouldest keep them from the evil" (John 17:15).

Anyone desisting from public sacrificial events was deemed unfit for political functions. Paul knew this and encouraged Christians to avoid politics altogether.

Paul wasn't the only Apostle running into this evangelism problem for Peter spoke of it as well: "For the time past of our life may suffice us to have wrought the will of the Gentiles, when we walked in … banqueting, and abominable idolatries: wherein they think it strange that ye run not with them to the same excess … speaking evil of you …" (1 Peter 4:3, 4).

Prior to Christianity, the Gentiles had eaten any and everything they desired, oblivious of any food laws. Becoming Christian meant putting an end to sacrificing to the gods their neighbours worshiped, and all former pagan god services as well as ceasing from eating foods declared to be unclean.

Paul expected Christians who turned from idols to create boundaries where there were none before. Paul is fully aware that living out this stiff position in a world of idols is likely to provoke alienation, resentment, and abuse. In this context Paul offers the heartening words: "There hath no temptation taken you but such as is common to man: but God is faithful, who will not suffer you to be tempted above that ye are able …" (1 Cor. 10:13).

FOODS SOLD AT MARKET

So prevalent was idol worship that it was difficult to find flesh food in the heathen communities that had not been sacrificed to idols. Most idol foods were of the clean meat variety: "Then the priest of Jupiter … brought oxen …" (Acts 14:13).

The idea that some animals are dangerous or disgusting is present in almost all known human cultures. The idolatrous Greeks of Paul's day regarded the pig as an animal in need of serious cleansing. Before the Greeks sacrificed a pig, they washed it and themselves in the sea. To think Paul went to extreme lengths to change the Christian Greeks viewpoint on eating pigs when there were so many other important beliefs to be learned is ridiculous indeed.

Paul anticipates potential problems presented by food that a Christian might purchase from the market by giving leave to eat anything without investigating its origins or history. Christ has not called believers to be meat inspectors therefore all food outside of the idol's orbit is permitted, be it flesh or vegetables. The food's past history only matters when it matters to someone else who considers it sacred. **"Whatsoever is sold in the shambles** (the market) **that eat …"** (1 Cor. 10:25). But then Paul adds to his counsel: **"… Asking no question for conscience sake"** (1 Cor. 10:25).

Paul is concerned for the believer's conscience and asking questions about the food's history in the open market would unnecessarily burden the seller's conscience as well. Idol food is always forbidden to Christians, however, they need not abstain from all food on the premise that it might earlier have been sacrificed to idols.

One can sense the fine line Paul is walking with the Corinthians. He desires them to adhere to the Council at Jerusalem, yet he does not want to lose them over this issue. So, Paul clarifies that food is food and permissible to eat unless it is specifically identified as idol food, which places it in a special forbidden category. Buy your meat at market and do not cause a stir by asking whether it was sacrificed to idols. Go home and enjoy your meal without conscience, without brooding over your decisions. Idol food is not dangerous outside of its overtly idolatrous context. In this case, ignorance is bliss. He counsels them to buy and eat whatever they like and can afford. On the other hand, if the buyer was informed that the purchase was idol food, then Paul insists that one must abstain for conscience sake.

FOODS OFFERED AT A FEAST

The rabbis absolutely forbade direct or indirect contact with pagan rites, but they ruled that Jews could intermingle with Gentiles unless it became clear that they were engaged in some religious activity. They assumed individuals could discern when the Gentile was engaged in idolatrous practices. Christians may discern all is well and need not become sleuths trying to detect if the food has idolatrous connections.

Instead, they may depend on the pagan's own pronouncement—This is sacred food. When Christians find themselves in this situation, then they must abstain from eating lest they be drawn into idolatry.

Even if sacred food were not consumed, the location of the banquet would cast its idolatrous shadow on the meal. Diners could not eat in such a place without a heightened consciousness of the gods. How could one eat in Demeter's sanctuary and not be reminded by word, symbol or ritual act, that the fruit of fertile ground was her gift? The god or gods were honoured by the meal and were conceived as being present. Often the food and fellowship would be explicitly set apart for religious rites.

Their willing consumption of what has been announced as food sacrificed to idols would:

(1) Compromise their confession of the One God with a blatant recognition of the sanctity of pagan gods making their censure seem hypocritical.

(2) It would confirm, rather than challenge, the unbeliever's idolatrous convictions and would not lead the unbeliever away from the worship of false gods. If a Christian were to eat what a pagan acquaintance regards as an offering to a deity, it would signal the Christian's endorsement of such idolatry.

Christians might avoid overt associations with idolatry by declining to attend meals connected to idols and their shrines, but what were they to do when they were guests at someone's house and offered food sacrificed to an idol? They had colleagues, relatives, and patrons who were devotees of other gods and goddesses, and they would be put in socially awkward situations when invited to another's home by a religiously minded host. Sacred food could be taken from the temple precincts and consumed at home, or religious rites could be performed over the food giving the meal a special character. The rites performed over the food were of significance and called for authentic thanksgiving to the gods.

"If any of them that believe not bid you to a feast, and ye be disposed to go; whatsoever is set before you, eat, asking no question for conscience sake" (1 Cor. 10:27). If an unbelieving idol worshipper invites you to dinner, and you accept, do not commence by asking questions as to whether this food or that has been previously sacrificed to idols. Not only will this insult the host, but it will put you in an unenviable position of turning down foods unnecessarily, causing further tension. The fact Paul says *"if ye be disposed to go"* indicates these invitations should not be an automatic yes and as you grow in your Christian walk there will be times in which you should decline such invitations.

"But if any man say unto you, 'This is offered in sacrifice unto idols, eat not ...'" (1 Cor. 10:28). Here is Paul's simple rule of faith. Once you know the food has been declared to be a sacrifice to the gods, your duty as a Christian is to leave it alone, without exception. If the idol food announcement is made in the midst of a meal, then this food should be left untouched regardless of how the hosts react.

COMPROMISE

Paul goes out of his way to be politically incorrect on this matter of compromise. He is more concerned about offending a jealous God, who claims sovereignty over all aspects of Christian life, than offending those who honour competing gods. Paul is concerned about the wrong message that tolerance might convey to those who are not followers of Christ.

The Corinthians made compromises and justified them. The lure of pagan society was strong with the idolaters' coaxing, *"Come and intermingle with us."* It is not surprising newly converted Christians would have bent under this significant pull to compromise with idolatrous practices. Anything that smacks of compromise, no matter how it might be rationalized, was to be rejected. Dissociating themselves from all overtly idolatrous celebrations demanded of the Corinthians an uncompromising devotion.

FUTURE OF THE CHURCH

Although practically meaningless to us today, of utmost importance was the practice of eating foods sacrificed to these idols by the Corinthians. They exhibited resistance to obey Paul and adhere to the Council from Jerusalem.

Of all the challenges Paul faced, eating foods sacrificed to idols was the most pressing, for the future of the Christian church hung in the balance. Consider there may not be a Christian church today had the new believers in Corinth decided to turn their back on God's appointed messenger to the Gentiles and walk in the sparks of their own kindling.

Paul's lengthy Bible account appears repetitive, archaic and wearisome. However, his strenuous work amongst the Corinthians most likely saved our modern society from worshipping these ancient idols. Only Christianity has the power to overcome their delusions, as evidenced today by the continued idol worship in heathen lands which have not embraced the gospel appeal.

The Corinthians were given no call to board an ark, and no slavery in Egypt to escape bondage from. There is no Nebuchadnezzar ordering men to bow down to a golden image. It was a simple case of obedience to the gospel versus the traditions of the gods. It is clear that Paul did not write First and Second Corinthians, and the Book of Romans as a go ahead to eat abominable unclean foods, yet from out of these books come the majority of proof texts used by those trying to prove Christians can eat anything.

Paul Challenges Corinthians

The study of the unclean foods becomes much easier if we recognize that Jesus dealt with the tradition of the Pharisee's washing before eating and Paul dealt with foods being sacrificed to idols. With the exception of a few written words from Apostles Peter and John, this battle against idol worship and eating their foods was primarily Apostle Paul's with the full backing of the church.

When Paul left the Council at Jerusalem he walked straight into this hornets' nest.

At all costs, for safety's sake, and for the furtherance of the gospel, the Lord's counsel was to be heeded: **"Blessed are the peacemakers"** (Matt. 5:9). Paul implored new converts: **"If it be possible, as much as lieth in you, live peaceably with all men"** (Rom. 12:18). Paul knew all too well that things could be quite peaceful for witnessing then turn into life threatening danger in an instant, usually over idols offended. A new Christian was to walk a three-fold tightrope of supreme tact: **"Give none offence, neither to the Jews, nor to the Gentiles, nor to the church of God …"** (1 Cor. 10:32).

Modern pastors think they have trouble trying to please the congregation and its various factions. Paul refused to compromise. His brilliant plan had to satisfy the Pharisees, Jewish converts, Gentile Christians, Gentile idol worshippers, and the church in Jerusalem on this matter of eating foods sacrificed to idols. Judging by his converts, this matter of solving foods sacrificed to idols was Paul's greatest accomplishment as a pastor/administrator.

JEWS

It was almost unbearable to deal with persecution from the Jews over preaching Jesus. The Jews would have chastised Paul far worse had he announced a strange new liberty to eat foods forbidden by the clergy for thousands of years. However, there is not a word in the New Testament raised in protest by the scribes and Pharisees concerning the matter Paul allowing unclean foods.

GENTILES

Heathen Gentiles were a major obstacle with their exhaustive idol worship and everything following in its train. Should idolaters become insulted the threat of death was always imminent. Greek and Roman idols were their passion and all aspects of life revolved around them.

CHURCH

The church at Jerusalem had been somewhat suspicious of Paul ever since his conversion on Damascus Road. He was on probation with many leaders who monitored closely that his new-found freedom did not stray. The church at Corinth severely tested the mettle of this bold Apostle. Every strain of Paul's mind was challenged to reform a church whose members were practicing fornication, eating foods sacrificed to idols and full of blood.

Many converted Jews had reverted to circumcision and the laws of Moses to maintain their strong faith. They urged circumcision for Gentile believers as a test of faith. **"Many thousands of Jews there are which believe; and they are all zealous of the law"** (Acts 21:20). To think this fanatical multitude would be silent concerning Paul introducing unclean foods into the gospel is beyond belief.

Peter said within Paul's writings **"are some things hard to be understood …"** (2 Pet. 3:16) and of a certainty the exploration into the intricacies of idol worship foods versus Christianity is where **"deep calleth unto deep"** (Ps. 42:7). As Pastor Paul contemplates the enormity of this challenge before him (that of re-educating an entire civilization) one can almost see him plotting his strategy late into the night. Once he is ready, Paul comes at the Corinthians with six primary arguments:

(1) There is but One God.
(2) Learn from the wilderness example.
(3) Compare the sacred Lord's Supper.
(4) Our Creator of these foods.
(5) Eat for conscience sake.
(6) Eating as an act of worship.

Paul's thoughts are repetitive, and we list these verses in chronological order within each of his arguments. Paul ministered in Corinth for eighteen months beginning in AD 53 where he wrote the book, First Corinthians. In AD 58, Paul returned for three months and wrote the powerful book of Romans. The book Second Corinthians was written in AD 60 from Macedonia in response to favourable reports Paul received regarding the church in Corinth. Paul's conversation with the Corinthians over this issue is ongoing because some resisted his prohibitions. Regarding foods sacrificed to idols, Paul is like a tenacious bulldog grasping a bone and he will not let go until reformation has been achieved. From Paul's writings originate almost all the verses which Christians use to justify eating unclean foods, or should we narrow it down to the pig. Throughout his writings the question of eating unclean foods remains unthinkable for a Jew. Paul meticulously preaches against food sacrificed to idols, full of blood and strangled, as stipulated by the Council of Jerusalem for all new believers. These dietary acts were often accompanied by fornication during the feasts. In Paul's attempt to win over the Corinthians to the Council of Jerusalem creed he was very lenient to them. It was Paul's ultimate goal to have Gentile believers abandon these heathen feasts altogether.

Scholars who isolate verses from Paul's courageous stand at Corinth to justify eating unclean meats need our forgiveness for their shallow proclamations.

ONE GOD

Paul introduces the dispute over idol-food by establishing common ground: Christians know that God is One and idols have no existence despite their mass following.

"Now as touching things offered unto idols, we know that we all have knowledge …" (1 Cor. 8:1) This knowledge came from the Council of Jerusalem.

"As concerning therefore the eating of those things that are offered in sacrifice unto idols, we know that an idol is nothing in the world, and that there is none other God but One. For though there be that are called gods, whether they be in heaven or in earth (as there be gods many, and lords many). But to us there is but One God, the Father, of whom are all things, and we in Him; and One Lord Jesus Christ, by whom are all things, and we by Him" (1 Cor. 8:4–6).

Christ is not simply another god in the pantheon of gods whose favour they might need to curry. Paul believes that the key implication of their new-found faith in Christ as One Lord is their rejection of any semblance of allegiance to other lords and gods.

WILDERNESS EXAMPLE

The Corinthian resistance to yield to Paul's objection over having One God necessitates a lengthier, more subtle approach. He does not immediately denounce their position but chooses a more circuitous route that winds its way through various facets of the problem turning it this way and that in an attempt to convince them to flee idolatry.

Paul turns up the heat of his argument against idol food by applying Israel's demise in the Wilderness directly to the Christians of Corinth. Their fathers' tragic end in the desert highlights the peril the Corinthians risk by consorting with devils. Paul reasons that violating the obligations given at Jerusalem and putting the Lord to the test would be suicidal.

"Moreover brethren, I would not that ye should be ignorant, how that all our fathers were under the cloud, and all passed through the sea; and all were baptized unto Moses in the cloud and in the sea. And did all drink the same spiritual drink: for they drank of that spiritual Rock that followed them: and that Rock was Christ" (1 Cor. 10:1–4).

In spite of the pre-Advent presence of Christ, and a type of baptism, the fathers failed to enter the Promised Land because of their idolatry. Their fall is a direct warning to the Corinthians since Paul underscores that these Scriptures apply directly to them.

"Now these things were our examples, to the intent that we should not lust after evil things, as they also lusted … Now all these things happened unto them for ensamples: and they are written for our admonition, upon whom the ends of the world are come" (1 Cor. 10:6, 11).

The children of Israel were an example to the Corinthians. The Corinthians as well as the children of Israel are given as an example to modern Christians.

"Neither be ye idolaters, as were some of them; as it is written, The people sat down to eat and drink, and rose up to play" (1 Cor. 10:7).

Paul quotes this Old Testament verse showing the futility of eating and drinking before an idol while attempting to ignore deity worship. Idolatry for Paul is a matter of eating cultic meals in an idol's presence.

"Neither let us commit fornication, as some of them committed, and fell in one day three and twenty thousand" (1 Cor. 10:8). From the days of Moses right through the Council at Jerusalem and into the world of the Gentiles, fornication and eating foods sacrificed to idols are deserving of the same fate. Lusting and eating often occurred during the same event.

"Neither let us tempt Christ, as some of them also tempted, and were destroyed of serpents" (1 Cor. 10:9). Paul warns the Corinthians if they dally at pagan feasts they can expect the same fate as Israel experienced in the wilderness. **"They shall not enter into My rest"** (Heb. 3:11).

"Wherefore, my dearly beloved, flee from idolatry" (1 Cor. 10:14). The bold Corinthians may not fear the power of idols, but they should fear the wrath of God. It is not their place to complain that being forbidden from participating in idol feasts places them in a difficult position. Paul implores the Corinthians to see the theological implications of this estranging behaviour.

THE LORD'S SUPPER

The Lord's Supper is a sacred meal that creates a fellowship of believers in the worship of Christ who is considered to be present. Pagan meals represent and create a fellowship of worshipers of pagan deities who are also considered to be present. Idols represent the realm of the demonic. Participating in the Lord's meal precludes participating in the other. Believers should not fool themselves into thinking that they are strong enough to affiliate with Christ and demons. To merge the two only kindles the jealousy and judgment of God.

"The cup of blessing which we bless, is it not the communion of the blood of Christ? The bread which we break, is it not the communion of the body of Christ? For we being many are one bread, and one body: for we are all partakers of that one bread" (1 Cor. 10:16–17). If you were a Corinthian, listening eagerly to an impassioned Paul, would you not be ashamed by partaking of idol foods?

> *Believers should not fool themselves into thinking that they are strong enough to affiliate with Christ and demons. To merge the two only kindles the jealousy and judgment of God*

"But I say, that the things which the Gentiles sacrifice, they sacrifice to devils, and not to God: and I would not that ye should have fellowship with devils. Ye cannot drink the cup of the Lord, and the cup of devils: ye cannot be partakers of the Lord's table, and of the table of devils" (1 Cor. 10:20–21).

The words of Joshua echo down through the ages, *"Choose you this day whom ye will serve"* (Josh. 24:15).

GOD IS CREATOR

"What say I then? That the idol is anything, or that which is offered in sacrifice to idols is anything?" (1 Cor. 10:19). Paul refuses to admit for a second that heathen idols have one iota of power within themselves. To answer the question how a Christian can act with integrity in a world brimming with idols, Paul moves from an absolute prohibition, based on the dangers of associating with anything known to be idolatrous, to conditional liberty based on a Biblical tenet: **"For the earth is the Lord's and the fullness thereof"** (1 Cor 10:26). Many jump at this text to prove you can eat anything, however, this verse is a word-for-word lift from Psalms 24:1 and certainly King David never gave credence to eating unclean foods. Outside of its idolatrous context, idol food is simply food and belongs to the One God. It is not permanently poisoned.

"For the earth is the Lord's, and the fullness thereof" (1 Cor. 10: 28). Paul repeats this Old Testament text for emphasis (Deut. 10:14). Paul's counsel to the Corinthians is in harmony with God's words to Noah after the flood: **"Every moving thing that liveth shall be meat for you; even as the green herb have I given you all things"** (Gen. 9:3).

One slightly used argument by proponents of those eating swine is that God divided the animals on the ark into clean and unclean strictly for sacrificial purposes.

Some theologians teach:

(1) God allowed Noah (a Gentile heir of righteousness by faith) to eat unclean foods.

(2) Abraham (a Jewish heir of righteousness by faith) to eat unclean foods.

(3) Moses (a Jewish heir of righteousness by faith) to put an end to eating unclean foods.

(4) Jesus (the Jewish fulfillment of righteousness by faith) to follow Moses' practice of not eating unclean foods.

(5) Paul (a Jewish heir of righteousness by faith) to introduce eating unclean foods to Jewish converts (heirs of righteousness by faith) for the first time in their history.

(6) Gentile believers make no changes from their previous heathen diet and continue to eat unclean foods.

Such is the folly of using Genesis 9:3 as a proof text that all foods are clean and that the animals boarded by sevens on the ark were for sacrificial purposes only. It also brings up the point as to why would Paul labour intently to convince the Gentile believers to eat unclean foods if they were already eating them.

"**I know, and am persuaded by the Lord Jesus, that there is nothing unclean of itself: but to him that esteemed any thing to be unclean to him it is unclean**" (Rom. 14:14). There are many instances in the Old Testament where situations not regarding forbidden foods are referred to as being *unclean*. Paul uses the term *unclean* to describe the immoral practice of eating idol foods. In this case, Paul refers to believers eating foods that have not been declared sacrificed to idols even though there is a probability they may have been. It affects each one differently as to whether your meal may have been contaminated by idolatrous circumstance. If eating questionable food affects your mental state—then don't.

"**All things indeed are pure; but it is evil for that man who eateth with offence**" (Rom. 14:20). It is impossible to taint a clean food although it is a different story if the food is known to have been sacrificed to imaginary gods. The first half of this verse is used frequently as an unclean food proof text. How is it possible to eat a pure food with offence? How can eating a pure food from God be described as an evil act? Obviously this verse does not refer to unclean meats.

FOR CONSCIENCE SAKE

"**Howbeit there is not in every man that knowledge: for some with conscience of the idol unto this hour eat it as a thing offered unto an idol; and their conscience being weak is defiled**" (1 Cor. 8:7). It is worthwhile to note what Paul defines as being weak—a person who eats foods sacrificed to idols. He is speaking to Corinthian church members possessing full knowledge of what is at stake in continuing this practice—foods coupled with fornication.

"**But meat commendeth us not to God: for neither, if we eat, are we the better; neither, if we eat not, are we the worse**" (1 Cor. 8:8). Paul, the supreme teacher of righteousness by faith, claimed no creature merit was earned from abstinence of idol foods, just as eating it won no favour with imaginary gods. For those unable to handle watching or partaking with a fellow Christian eating food that may have been previously sacrificed to idols:

"**But take heed lest by any means this liberty of your's becomes a stumbling block to them that are weak**" (1 Cor 8:9).

Paul now appeals to those who think they are strong enough to not be affected by eating foods sacrificed to idols. He warns them of being the cause of weaker brethren to fall. **"For if any man see thee which hast knowledge sit at meat in the idol's temple, shall not the conscience of him which is weak be emboldened to eat those things which are offered to idols; And through thy knowledge shall the weak brother perish, for whom Christ died?"** (1 Cor. 8:10). Paul states how serious a matter this is: **"But when ye sin so against the brethren, and wound their weak conscience, ye sin against Christ"** (1 Cor. 8:12).

Paul now concludes this portion of his argument in the spirit of Moses who loved his brethren so much that he told the Lord in order to save them: **"Blot me ... out of Thy book ..."** (Exod. 32:32). It is in harmony of spirit with Paul saying, **"I could wish that myself were accursed from Christ for my brethren, my kinsmen ..."** (Rom. 9:3). Paul would fast himself to death before causing a believer to stumble. **"Wherefore, if meat make my brother to offend, I will eat no flesh while the world standeth, lest I make my brother to offend"** (1 Cor. 8:13). Some theologians have concluded this text is talking about how weak vegetarians are but these comments are so ridiculous as to not warrant further discussion.

On Paul's subsequent trip to the Corinthians, when he wrote the Book of Romans, he repeats an earlier theme on subject of foods sacrificed to idols: **"Let us not ... put a stumbling block or an occasion to fall in his brother's way"** (Rom. 14:13). Above all else in the maze of considering idol foods, your brother comes first.

"But if thy brother be grieved with thy meat, now walkest thou not charitably. Destroy not him with thy meat ... Let not then your good be evil spoken of" (Rom. 14:13–16). Paul warns that a fellow believer could be destroyed if you were to callously eat without regard for his spiritual condition. Even if this subject were talking about the unclean foods of Leviticus, how many Christians who eat pork are concerned about the spiritual welfare of their fellow believers who choose not to eat it? The opposite is true, for pork eaters flaunt their misguided liberty in the face of those who don't eat it—then call them legalists. This is as far from Paul's counsel as the east is from the west.

Paul puts this issue of eating foods sacrificed to idols in its proper prospective: **"It is good neither to eat flesh ... nor any thing whereby thy brother stumbleth, or is offended, or is made weak"** (Rom. 14:21). Paul is ever cognizant of causing another to fall from grace. He will fast before doing so.

"All things are lawful for me, but all things are not expedient: all things are lawful for me, but all things edify not" (1 Cor. 10:23). Paul implies a Christian has the liberty to do all things without being affected by it, but it is not wise to do so for fear of hurting the weak. He says if he should do these things it does not edify the church, so he will not do them. God comes first in all matters of conscience. You do what is right because it is right. To think this solitary verse in the midst of Paul's elaborate preaching sanctions eating unclean foods is an embarrassment to any seeker of truth. At no point beginning at First Corinthians 8 and into chapter 10 was there a single inference of introducing unclean meats into the picture.

"Eat not for his sake that shewed it, and for conscience sake" (1 Cor 10:28). This matter is about the believer being a witness in all he does.

"Conscience, I say, not thine own, but of the other ..." (1 Cor. 10:29). Ever aware of the possibility of winning a soul over from idolatry unto Christ, Paul states why it is so important to set a proper example of refusing to eat foods sacrificed unto strange gods. One might question why Paul was so concerned with the conscience of idolaters? He looked at a bigger picture than just strengthening Gentile believers. In Paul's thought process, this gospel was going to convert the entire world, including idol worshippers. "Even as I please all men in all things, not seeking mine own profit, but the profit of many, that they may be saved" (1 Cor 10:33).

"For why is my liberty judged of another man's conscience? For if I by grace be a partaker, why am I evil spoken of for that for which I give thanks?" (1 Cor. 10:29, 30).

Many Christians use this text to defend themselves from Christians who don't believe in eating unclean foods, thus placing this verse far from context. Unclean foods were not the issue in Paul's day. Who was it that judged Gentile believers eating at the feasts of unbelievers? It was the Jews, both converted and unconverted. They were struggling because the gospel was brought to the Gentiles without stipulations other than eating foods sacrificed to idols or strangled with blood. The sight of Gentile Christians eating with heathens was too much for the Jews to bear.

With agape love Paul spoke to the Corinthians, allowing men a freedom of choice whether they wished to partake of foods that might have been sacrificed to idols: "He that eateth, eateth to the Lord, for he giveth God thanks; and he that eateth not, to the Lord he eateth not, and giveth God thanks" (Rom. 14:6).

EATING AS A FORM OF WORSHIP

"For the kingdom of God is not meat and drink; but righteousness, and peace, and joy in the Holy Ghost ... Let us therefore follow after the things which make for peace, and things wherewith one may edify another. For meat destroy not the work of God" (Rom. 14:17, 19, 20).

There has been too much time, too many words spent on this subject when Christians elsewhere were dying as martyrs for Jesus Christ. One can sense Paul is weary of this topic, anxious to move on to the weightier matters of the gospel: **"Happy is he that condemneth not himself in that thing which he alloweth"** (Rom. 14:22). The key to peace on this matter is to follow Paul's outline which is based upon the simple command from the Jerusalem Council.

"And he that doubteth is damned if he eat, because he eateth not of faith: for whatsoever is not of faith is sin" (Rom. 14:23). If you feel condemned eating foods that might have been sacrificed to idols, for conscience sake, do not do it. If you cannot eat in fullness of faith, then you must not eat it at all, lest it become a matter of sin for doubting that the food was approved by God.

In modern perspective, if a person feels he can only eat organic, and to eat foods non-organic would cause sickness and death, then one could will himself into sickbay just by thinking he is eating contamination. A chocolate freak, who feels he is gaining weight with every bite, should leave the chocolate to one who can actually enjoy it. Neither one of these instances compare fully to the idol food issue which was declared by Jerusalem to be an open act of sin.

"Whether therefore ye eat, or drink, or whatsoever ye do, do all to the glory of God" (1 Cor. 10:31). Paul introduces a new thought for all Christians—eating is an act of worship! As much as worshipping in the temple, how we conduct ourselves at the dinner table is an act of glorifying the Lord. The cross of Christ is stamped on every loaf of bread. If every meal is the Lord's provisional gift of supper, how does the thought of eating unclean foods sit in your heart? To whom do you offer worship with each meal?

Paul's ministry had borne much fruit and obedience. His tone changed. No longer was the issue concerning which foods to eat and how to eat them but in his following letter appeals to the Corinthians to take the next step and forgo idols entirely. **"Be ye not unequally yoked together with unbelievers; for what fellowship hath righteousness with unrighteousness? And what communion hath light with darkness? And what concord hath Christ with Belial? Or what part hath he that believeth with an infidel? And what agreement hath the temple of God with idols? For ye are the temple of the living God ... Wherefore come out from among them and be ye separate, saith the Lord, and touch not the unclean thing; and I will receive you"** (2 Cor. 6:14–17). If the previous comments of Paul had been giving the green light to eat unclean foods, then what strange counsel he would be giving two years later telling the same believers not to touch the unclean things. Of course he wasn't talking about unclean Bible foods, but idol foods.

EPISTLE OF PAUL TO TITUS

Titus was a Gentile convert of Paul who had charge of the church on the Isle of Crete when this book was written in AD 65.

"**Unto the pure all things are pure …**" (Titus 1:15). In most discussions regarding unclean food this text is paraded out as proof you can eat anything. In the short book of Titus, the subject of food is not even discussed. Paul is comparing believers with those of the circumcision, whether they are believing Jews or unbelieving.

Paul repeats the thought of Jesus that a genuine gospel follower can be counted on to live a pure and holy life. Compare this to those religious zealots around them who were "**… giving heed to Jewish fables, and commandments of men …**" (Titus 1:14). Paul is not addressing God's laws here, but the countless and useless commandments of men that both he and Jesus rebuked the Jews sternly for following.

"**But unto them that are defiled and unbelieving is nothing pure … they profess that they know God; but … being abominable, and disobedient, and unto every good work reprobate**" (Titus 1:15–16). Paul speaks of enemies of the pure gospel of righteousness by faith as being abominable and disobedient. Are we to believe Paul would use these terms to describe those who adhere to the dietary laws of Moses? This is out of harmony with his continual reasoning that we should never be a stumbling block to others.

MODERN PRACTICE

Over time, Paul's ministry and the power of Christianity literally destroyed heathen worship in the known Greek and Roman world. Europe and North America are civilizations patterned after the Greco-Roman systems—education, medical, government, transportation, and social habits are modern mirrors of these ancient superpowers—minus the idols. It is not a stretch to surmise that Paul's incredible ministry saved us from living within a system of ancient idol worship and eating foods sacrificed to their deities.

Pressures to conform have not changed for Christians today living in cultures where food is regularly offered to one god or another. Some of the largest world religions are heavily involved in foods sacrificed to idols because there are no preachers to lay down the gospel arguments Paul used. In their quest for liberty, missionaries believe Paul's elaborate message is strictly for the allowance of eating pork. They journey to distant islands armed with the gospel but miss the boat on the message of Paul to Asia Minor. Mighty civilizations whom Paul never had contact with were left to indulge in their heathen ways resulting in gigantic world religions mocking Christianity at every level. Score a triumph for Satan as cultish ties regarding diet and tradition remain so influential in our world.

Is not a revival possible should one use Paul's methods? Many today are concerned not to cause offence, and toleration of other faiths has become the watchword. As infiltration of these world religions continue to permeate Western society through immigration, this battle over foods sacrificed to idols is not over. In Christianity's current theological state we are powerless to halt the growing reoccurrence of idol worship and offering food sacrifices to them.

HINDUISM [3,200 BC and onward]

Before sitting for food, the place is purified and the articles of food are served in a leaf. Before taking the food, a little water is sprinkled while adherents repeat chants. This repetition purifies the food. Then a little water is sipped. The food is offered daily to five deities before the worshipper partakes of it. Taking food also can be converted into an act of Yoga or sacrifice. He should say:" "I offer to Thee, this food which belongs to Thee only." The custom of the Hindus is that they feed the guest who comes to their house before they take food.

There are an estimated 885 million Hindus (13% of world's population), making this the world's third largest religion.

BUDDHISM [AD 200 and onward]

To father and mother Buddha, two pieces of food in triangular shape are offered—white for vegetarian gods and red for carnivorous gods. Mustard seeds are brought to drive away evils. Five kinds of grain are also brought along with numerous red apples or bananas.

There are estimated 350 million Buddhists (6% of world's population), making this the world's fourth largest religion.

In China, to advise the Chinese not to eat the food in ancestor worship may be implicitly advising them not to love their parents, nor practice love, and ultimately not to be Chinese.

OTHER WORLD RELIGIONS

The Muslims (at 20% of the world's population and growing), follow God's prescribed dietary laws and do not sacrifice to idols, nor eat foods containing blood.

Judaism (at 1% of the world population) continue to follow God's dietary plan.

Christianity (at 32% of the world's population and dropping) follow the heathen format of eating foods containing blood and all manner of unclean beasts.

CLOSING THOUGHTS ON PAUL

For Paul to write the equivalent of three books of the Bible trying to convince the Gentile Christians they should eat unclean foods (1 Corinthians 8 and 10; 2 Corinthians 6; Romans 14 and other places) makes absolutely no sense if these new converts came from a previous lifestyle which allowed them to eat all manner of unclean. A bigger question may be this: if Gentile Christians needed to be converted from eating unclean foods, why is there no mention of Paul's preaching on this subject? In the same manner there is no mention of Paul preaching that these new believers needed to keep a day of rest, for this was completely foreign to them as well. Whether you believe Paul taught them that the first day of the week was the new Sabbath or that the traditional seventh day was the Sabbath—it makes no difference—Paul mentions it in passing but there are no chapters in the New Testament devoted to this subject. When a new convert came over from idolatry there would be changes in worship patterns and in diet. Paul taught them to honour their father and mothers, to stop bearing false witness and coveting. All the Commandments are mentioned in passing but not focused on as worthy of entire recorded sermons.

Food sacrificed to idols is not an issue amongst Western society Christians, therefore texts regarding food have been grossly misinterpreted. Paul's writings have been boiled down to a solitary purpose—allowing a tiny percentage of unclean meat, fish and fowl to adorn the tables of Christians. In Paul's final trip to Jerusalem, James sums up the amazing success of Paul: *"They keep themselves from things offered to idols"* (Acts 21:25).

Sadly, Christians are blinded from recognizing the utter destruction of idol worship through the painstaking efforts of Apostle Paul. His ministry not only launched the Christian church, but we can praise God for not being surrounded everywhere by ancient pagan idol gods. Christians are no longer challenged by conforming to society's peer pressure even under the threat of death.

New Testament Prophecy

1 TIMOTHY 4

The book of First Timothy was written in AD 64, after Paul's initial bouts with the Corinthians.

"Now the Spirit speaketh expressly, that in the latter times some shall depart from the faith, giving heed to seducing spirits, and doctrines of devils. Speaking lies in hypocrisy; having their conscience seared with a hot iron" (1 Tim. 4:2). The apostles believed they were living in the last times so these words have a dual application. Paul was used by God not only as His greatest theologian but also as an important prophet. **"For every creature of God is good, and nothing to be refused, if it be received in thanksgiving"** (1 Tim. 4:4).

Paul had cautioned the Corinthians to be mindful of offending a brother over the issue of foods. He had said that he would fast unto death before offending them. Are we to believe within four years he changed his focus to the point of now lambasting those who refuse to eat unclean foods as being liars and hypocrites? Paul spent days talking about the valuable conscience of believers and unbelievers on this issue. Is he now saying those who refuse to allow unclean foods have no conscience, and are transformed into seducing spirits and devils? Paul never wavered, just like the God he served who says: **"I am the Lord, I change not ..."** (Mal. 3:6).

"For it is sanctified by the word of God and prayer" (1 Tim. 4:5). *Sanctify* is a word meaning to make holy or set apart for a right use or purpose—in this case to set apart as fit for human food. The only passages in Scripture showing which meats God sanctified are found in Leviticus 11 and Deuteronomy 14. God's clean, healthful meats are identified by name to be received with thanksgiving and prayer. No unclean creature is ever identified by name as being fit to eat—snails, oysters, clams, snakes, octopuses, eels, horses or swine—only negative connotations relating to Babylon and rebellion. In Judaism, the prayer voiced before a meal affirms that God is sovereign over all things and that everything created by God is good. The whole creation belongs to God, not part to God and part to idols. Idol food therefore loses its character as soon as it leaves the idol's arena and the idolater's purposes. Once blessed by prayer, clean food cannot become unclean food if by chance it happened to be sacrificed to imaginary gods.

"Forbidding to marry and commanding to abstain from meats, which God hath created to be received with thanksgiving of them which believe and know the truth." (1 Tim. 4:2, 3). In Paul's day there were sects who practiced celibacy along with fasting from clean meats especially concerning the sixth day of the week when Jesus was crucified.

Middle Age reformers pounced on this verse to identify their deathly foe, the beast of Revelation. Men like Huss, Luther, and Meno Simon, questioned their affiliation with the universal world church, and these verses helped to identify a movement which forbad marriage of their priests and urged their members to refrain from eating clean meats on Friday (as a penance to commemorate Christ's death), a practice continuing unto this day among many in the world's largest church. Clean meats which to abstain from are defined by the Roman church as the flesh of any warm-blooded animal, thus their allowance of fish.

"No one can marry after he has been ordained priest" (First Council of Nicea, AD 314).

"Throughout the Latin Church, the law of abstinence prohibits all responsible subjects from indulging in meat diet on duly appointed days ... according to the appreciation of intelligent and law-abiding Christians" (*Catholic Encyclopedia*—Abstinence).

It is interesting to note that during these times of forced abstinence, the following cold blooded, unclean animals were permitted to be eaten by this ecclesiastic power: *"For this reason, the use mollusks, crabs, turtles, frogs, and such like cold-blooded creatures is not at variance with the law of abstinence"* (*Catholic Encyclopedia*—Abstinence).

> *This time of ignorance God has winked at but now calls every discerner of truth to be nourished in words of faith and good doctrine*

If thou put the brethren in remembrance of these things, thou shalt be a good minister of Jesus Christ, nourished up in the words of faith and of good doctrine, whereunto thou has attained" (1 Tim. 4:4–6). There are many good ministers of Christ who have isolated Paul's writings of

1 Timothy chapter 4 out of context thus encouraging their members to eat unclean foods. This time of ignorance God has winked at but now calls every discerner of truth to be nourished in words of faith and good doctrine.

JOHN THE REVELATOR [AD 96]

John had been likely present at the Council of Jerusalem when the decree went forth regarding two vital matters on health for new Christians (blood and idols). Years after Paul's death, eating foods sacrificed to idols is still an issue with believers just as it had always been with Old Testament Israel.

The seven churches of Revelation refer to seven historical periods in Christian history, but in plurality John was also writing to the seven literal churches of his day located in the province of Asia Minor.

"To the angel of the church in Pergamos write ... thou holdest fast My name, and hast not denied My faith ... but I have a few things against thee, because thou hast there them that hold the doctrine of Balaam ... to eat things sacrificed to idols ..." (Rev. 2:12–14). By New Testament times, Baal worship had progressed from sacrificing children to idols to eating foods sacrificed to idols.

"And unto the angel of the church in Thyatira write ... I know thy works, and charity and service, and faith, and thy patience ... notwithstanding I have a few things against thee, because thou sufferest that woman Jezebel, which calleth herself a prophetess, to teach and to seduce My servants to commit fornication, and to eat things sacrificed to idols" (Rev. 2:18–20).

Should doubts arise regarding the mercy of God and His longsuffering, one need look no further than to the churches at Pergamos and Thyatira who still had among them those who were disobeying the direct command from Jerusalem regarding idols and fornication. This was in spite of the extensive ministry of Apostle Paul forty years prior to John's writing.

None of These Diseases

"If thou wilt diligently hearken to the voice of the LORD thy God, and wilt do that which is right in His sight, and wilt give ear to His commandments, and keep all His statutes, I will put none of the diseases upon thee, which I have brought upon the Egyptians: for I am the LORD that healeth thee" (Exod. 15:26).

"Thou shalt therefore keep the commandments, and the statutes, and the judgements, which I command thee this day, to do them ... And the LORD will take away from thee all sickness, and will put none of the evil diseases of Egypt, which thou knowest, upon thee; but will lay them upon all them that hate thee" (Deut. 7:11, 15).

The warning concerning disobedience to God is indeed fearful: "If thou wilt not observe to do all the words of this law that are written in this book, that thou mayest fear this glorious and fearful name, THE LORD THY GOD; Then the Lord will make thy plagues wonderful, and the plagues of thy seed, even great plagues, and of long continuance. Moreover He will bring upon thee all the diseases of Egypt, which thou wast afraid of; and they shall cleave unto thee" (Deut. 28:58–60).

What were the diseases of Egypt to be feared and which would result through disobedience to an all-wise and loving God? The Egyptians were notorious for eating unclean foods. Autopsies performed on ancient Egyptians show their bodies riddled with all the latest diseases of today's Western society. Information in *Chamber's Medical Encyclopaedia,* under the heading "Worm Infestation in Man" may enlighten us to some extent: "Our knowledge of the existence and effects of such parasites goes back in the case of man, to Egyptian papyri of about 1,500 BC. These contain accounts of *anaemia* [deficiency of the hemoglobin, often accompanied by a reduced number of red blood cells and causing pallor, weakness, and breathlessness] leaving little doubt its cause was *ancylostomiasis* [a lethargic anaemic state due to blood loss through the feeding of hookworms in the small intestine]."

Today one of the great medical problems of Egypt is the control of the *helminth infection* [a parasitic worm, such as a tapeworm, that parasitizes the intestine of a vertebrate]. It causes *Schistosomiasis* [worms transmitted to humans through feces-contaminated fresh water or snails] characterized by infection and gradual destruction of the tissues of the kidneys, liver, and other organs. Worms attain maturity, and cause much of their injury through hemorrhage and damage to tissue resulting from the passage of eggs to the intestine and bladder whence they start a new cycle of infection]. This is a historic problem proved by the finding of *schistosome eggs* in sections cut out from the tissues of the preserved pharaohs.

Yet even the ancient Egyptians regarded the pig as detestable. If they touched it casually, they at once plunged into water to purify themselves. RA said to the other gods, *"The pig will be abominable"* and they were never sacrificed to him. But Egyptians sacrificed swine to Osiris *"not that which is dear to the gods but that which is contrary is fit to be sacrificed."* The pig was eaten sacrificially once per year. If one of the most heathen nations in the history of the earth felt that way about the pig, calling it an abomination, how should modern Christians view the animal as food?

When the children of Israel obeyed God, wonderful were the results: **"He brought them forth ... and there was not one feeble person among their tribes"** (Ps. 105:37).

This is a great miracle for the estimated mixed multitude coming out of Egypt numbered between one and two million. Can you imagine even one thousand people in our society being completely illness free? When Moses led the people out of the land of Egypt, God reversed 400 years of very poor eating habits practiced while in captivity. Not only was a list of unclean animals given to Israel, but it was necessary to add strict rules and stipulations to accompany their revised eating habits and ensure sanitation in tough desert conditions.

TAPEWORM *[Cestoda]*

The dangerous pork tapeworm may grow from two to six yards long (*Chamber's*, v.3, p. 245). This animal sheds live segments of the worm. Each segment of a tapeworm can contain both a male and a female productive organ. These tapeworms are plainly visible and usually detected by meat inspectors. If not detected, they are hopefully killed by adequate cooking. According to some sources pig must be cooked almost black before there can be certainty the worms within have been destroyed. The pig is a dirty feeder and if infected, it is usually heavily infected and in need of serious de-worming. The eggs of this worm develop inside the pig and adult worms have been found alive, four weeks after the pig has been killed. Cold storage does not kill these worms. In humans, worm powders give only short-lived relief. If the worm dies or is removed, the damaged tissues can remain inflamed and open to invasion by other organisms or germs, producing further forms of disease, and possibly malignant growths.

Of wicked Herod it is written, **"The angel of the Lord smote him, because he gave not God the glory: and he was eaten of worms, and gave up the ghost"** (Acts 12:23).

CASE HISTORY

A young girl was suffering from epileptic defective muscular control. As an introduction to the case there is a short description of the common tape worm *[taenia solium]* found in the intestines of human beings. The child had shown various symptoms before being admitted to hospital, including attacks of pain, numbness in left arm and leg; vomiting; and twitching on the left side of her face. In hospital she at times experienced defective muscular control *[ataxic]*, resulting in irregular and jerky movements. After various tests, it was decided to give operative treatment. A total of thirty tapeworms in larvae state were found lying over the cortex, that is, the grey matter of the brain. The majority of these were so embedded that it was impossible to remove them. A few were attached to the outer membrane of the *meninges* which surrounds the brain and spinal cord and these were removed. This case history concludes with a forecast of likely recurrent attacks which may increase in both degree and frequency. The larva stage of the tape worm *[cysticerci]* would enlarge and multiply, and the child would in time be likely beyond medical or surgical help. This study concludes brain involvement with the *cysticerci* may give rise to epileptic fits (*Nursing Mirror*, June 3, 1960).

Reasons could be put forward as to why some pay the penalty and others appear not to when it comes to eating unclean foods. For every cigar smoking, whiskey drinking centurion, legions rest in the grave not so fortunate. A refuge wall of excuse for disobedience is built on the basis that thousands live long lives and never come to harm even though they eat the pig and its unclean accomplices. There comes a time when common sense has to preside when you study instance after instance in the Bible concerning the pig—and none of it is good! God created the pig as a useful scavenger—an ancient garbage disposal unit. It does its job well. Research has convinced some non-religious doctors and nutritionists to recommend that some of their patients avoid pork and shellfish strictly as a matter of health.

SHELLFISH

Devotees of shellfish hold no other food in such high esteem. However, no other food tends to be as contaminated by bacteria, viruses and toxins. Unfortunately, it is technically impossible to determine which shellfish are contaminated. The high risk has to do with how and where these creatures live and what they eat. As a group they are carrion eaters feeding primarily on dead and decaying animals, sea vultures cleansing the sea of organic waste. They tear up other aquatic animals with powerful pincers, choosing those who are sick or weak. They devour their own young.

By filtering large amounts of water, shellfish retain solid particles of pollutants. As God's pollution control devices, they harbor mercury, cadmium, and chemicals. Everything shellfish capture should be considered carcinogenic. Tens of millions of viruses are dumped into the seas daily containing billions of bacteria. Red tide is a sign of severe aquatic contamination. Shellfish provide an ideal medium for picking up foreign bacteria. The poisons on the bottom of the seas are passed from one carnivorous creature to the next increasing in toxicity as it moves up the food chain.

Shellfish are the most perishable food product with rapid decline after death. The boric acid solution used to maintain shellfish's rosy color and retard decay is also a toxic. Shellfish, together with swine, are the animals richest in free amino acids serving as pre-digested nutrients for germs.

Unclean foods are out of balance in regard to vitamin and mineral distribution. For example, a tiny amount of zinc is required each day by the human body to function effectively. Zinc can be picked up in a variety of simple ways, almost without trying, yet those who eat a plate of unclean mussels from the sea, ingest 3,500 times more zinc into their system than is required.

Howard B. Rand, in his book *Digest of the Divine Law,* makes the following comments:

"Wherever there is disease and sickness among God's people ... they are refusing to keep and administer His laws. Multitudes continue to live in pain and suffering, while countless numbers have gone to untimely graves for this national failure. Certain fundamental laws are given in the Bible, which, if kept, would give that health and vigour so characteristic of the life of Moses. Moses died at the age of one hundred and twenty years and the record states, 'His eye was not dim nor his natural force abated' (Deut. 34:7)."

The Jewish festival, Hanukkah, in Hebrew means *dedication*. It is a time of rejoicing for the Jewish people, because after their temple was defiled by the Syrian tyrant Antiochus Epiphanes, it was retaken and dedicated for holy use. Antiochus had desecrated the temple of God by placing an idol of Zeus in it and sacrificing a swine on the altar. The unclean hog was never an acceptable sacrifice to the Eternal God. Antiochus was not making an offering to the God of Israel and the presence of the blood of an unclean animal on the altar of God defiled the temple. After regaining control of their temple, the Jews removed the idol of Zeus, and painstakingly cleaned the swine blood off the altar. After this was accomplished, the temple was ready for rededication for the holy use of worshiping the Lord. This historical account took place in 165 BC. When God created the pig, He pronounced it good. But clearly it was not a good animal to sacrifice in the temple of God. Its very presence defiled the earthly dwelling place of God.

Today Christians are called the temple of God. "Know ye not that ye are the temple of God, and that the Spirit of God dwelleth in you? If any man defile the temple of God, him shall God destroy; for the temple of God is holy, which temple ye are" (1 Cor. 3:16–17).

If God did not want unclean animals in His dwelling place that Solomon built, then He doesn't want them in the dwelling place that Christ built, which is inside the Christian.

SINGLE STOMACH ANIMALS

Single stomached animals contrast with the four chambered stomachs of the clean animals. Creatures such as the horse, pig, and rabbit lack the purifying filter of the clean stomached animals. As a result their meat is more vulnerable to negative effects that their own feed may contain in terms of chemical composition, contaminants, and parasites. In other words, single stomach creatures lack divine protection when it comes to humans eating them.

If you enjoy pig meat, you would make a good cannibal for they are closest to human flesh. Pig valves are easily substituted into human hearts. Pigs are immunologically similar to humans (Wikipedia).

The pig will eat anything (omnivorous diet), thus their meat contains the most parasites. From a health standpoint there is more criticism focused on pork than any other meat. It is rich in a gelatinous material that infiltrates pork *[mucopolysaccharide]* and serves to support bacterial growth. The high free amino acid content in pork serves as pre-digested nutrients for germs.

> *From a health standpoint there is more criticism focused on pork than any other meat*

If the pig were a clean animal with multi-stomachs, many of their problems as food would disappear. To date, man has been unable to genetically create a four-chambered stomach pig, or even try, due to the fact that genetic scientists do not look to Bible for guidance.

Rabbits feed on their own excrement and frequently suffer from plagues. Their meat is rich in waste products and compounds such as urea which are generally toxic.

Horses are herbivore (vegetarian) but not ruminant. The horse can easily transmit trichinosis as does the swine.

If the rat was purified at Calvary's cross and remains a filthy flea-ridden scavenger, living in sewers and eating from cesspools—then why don't Christians eat it?

UNCLEAN FOOD DISEASES

ADDICTIONS

Pork contains plenty of *hypoxanthine* which is an addictive stimulant. Hypoxanthine has a chemical structure similar to caffeine or cocoa which are central nervous system stimulants. It produces a sensation of vitality and energy and is addictive, meaning it must be continued to avoid withdrawal symptoms.

ALLERGIES

Pork contains more histamine, which provokes allergies.

Mites are tiny insects that leave a yellowish dust on the surface of the ham, which cause respiratory allergies.

Shellfish cause allergies due to the amount of germs they contain.

ARTERIOSCLEROSIS

Consumption of pork fat is related to cardiovascular disease, such as arteriosclerosis, due to its high total fat, saturated fat, and cholesterol content.

ARTHRITIS

Consumption of pork is associated with increased levels of uric acid, which causes gout.

Shellfish is high in uric acid, synonymous with arthritic pain.

BRAIN/NERVOUS SYSTEM

Meningitis can be caused by sausage and cooked ham which can transmit this disease.

Cysticercosis occurs when pork tapeworms end up in the brain causing seizures, difficulty with balance, and swelling of the brain. Death can occur suddenly with heavy infections. It is transmitted from the feces eating swine and is almost non-existent in Muslim countries where pork is forbidden.

Children that eat one or more pork hot dogs per week have a 210% higher risk of brain tumors.

Consumption of processed pork (ham, bacon) increases the risk of cancer of the nervous system [*cerebral glioma*] due to the nitrosamine content of these foods.

CANCER

Consumption of pork is associated with various types of cancer due to pork's content of carcinogenic substances.

The greater the pork consumption in a country results in the higher the incidence of cervical cancer in women as shown in the following chart. Lymphoma is also linked to pork as it is known to be caused by a virus.

In curing or fermenting sausage, the following are added to the pork intestine: nitrites (to avoid putrefaction and give a bright color), sulfur dioxide (preservative), polyphosphates (retain moisture and tenderness), and glutamate (flavor enhancer). This causes excess fat accounting for 30–50% of its weight. Sausage consumption is related to various types of cancerous diseases. Bacon is the most unhealthful of all pork derivatives. It is more than half fat, cured with nitrates, and often smoked.

African-Americans consume more bacon, ham, and sausage than Euro-Americans or Hispanics. Subsequently, they have 20% more colon cancer and 50% more pancreatic cancer than their neighbors.

Among meats, pork is the main messenger of danger as studies show cancer causing mutagens begin forming during the first moments of frying.

Stewing meat in liquid creates juices which have attracted researchers to declare that dangerous sources, especially from pork, are found dissolved right into the broth, making it four times more dangerous than roast beef.

The following situations are severely agitated by the use of shellfish: Aids, lymphoma, malignant tumors, and patients undergoing chemotherapy.

(*Encyclopedia of Foods and Healing Power*, v.1, pp. 252–261).

CHOLERA

Pork provides the ideal medium for the cholera germ which can cause this devastating and sometimes lethal disease. Sources of contamination tend to be the butchers and cooks.

Cholera in developed countries is linked to consumption of raw oysters.

DIABETES

In a stunning revelation: for a diabetic to persist in eating shellfish this can eventually lead to blindness.

(*Encyclopedia of Foods and Healing Power*, v.1, pp. 252–261).

FLU

Swine are the natural reservoir of many viruses, including the one that causes flu in humans.

Pigs are also common vectors in transmission of the flu to humans from birds ("Bird Flu," Wikipedia).

Hog cholera or swine fever is a frequent epidemic in hog farms, killing many animals.

In severe viruses caused by eating shellfish, no amount of cooking, roasting, frying, or steaming can kill them.

HEART

Consumption of pork fat is related to cardiovascular disease, such as coronary heart disease, due to its high total fat, saturated fat, and cholesterol content.

Shellfish are high in cholesterol (2x that of beef).

HIGH BLOOD PRESSURE

Pork contains more tyramine, which produces hypertension, along with its high salt content.

INFECTIONS

Pork consumption can cause infections, especially in children and the elderly who are more susceptible.

Wounds infected by shellfish can result in amputation.

INTESTINAL

The pork worm *[trichinellia spiralis]*, the cause of trichinosis, is normally a parasite of the pig or the rat (*Chamber's Encyclopaedia*, v. 14, p. 742).

Main sources of trichinosis are from eating the unclean swine or bear which have been infected by the common rat.

At the slaughterhouse, pork must be microscopically examined to assure the absence of trichina parasites.

One gram of infested, inadequately cooked pork may contain as many as 3000 trichina larval cysts, both male and female.

The bug itself is transmitted to humans as a minute worm. Once inside the digestive system, the worms develop into adults and mate. Each pregnant female gives birth to thousands of live, young worms which gnaw through the small intestine and then travel via the bloodstream to the muscles, where they form cysts. Trichinosis is a progressive disease and may end in death.

The effects of trichinosis are wide-spread and hard to diagnose, the symptoms varying from so-called rheumatism, fever, anaemia, headaches, muscular paralysis, internal bleeding—and even blindness. It can lead to edema (swelling of face or eyelids). The Cornell Medical Center has revealed a very shocking statistic of which the Science Editor of the *New York Herald Tribune* describes as a national disgrace—trichinosis strikes about one out of every four persons at some time in their life.

Diarrhea is caused by eating raw, cured ham. A germ found in pus is often exposed during the slaughterhouse butchering process. Abscesses often existing on the swine's feet are inadvertently opened, often contaminating the carcass. This causes gastroenteritis.

LIVER

A 1985 study found a significant correlation between cirrhosis and pork consumption from its high content of nitrogenous compounds which must be metabolized in the liver. The risk obviously increases combined with alcohol usage (A. Nanji, S. French).

Hepatitis A from wastewater can remain alive in the sea for up to a year and commonly infects shellfish.

Hepatitis C may never be fully cured and is strongly linked to eating raw seafood.

It is strongly recommended that patients undergoing renal dialysis avoid shellfish at all costs. Shellfish is an enemy making worse cases of liver disease and alcoholism.

PARASITES

Pork is the meat with the highest incidence of parasites. Trichinosis, cysticercosis, and toxoplasmosis are some of the parasitic diseases contracted from pork.

PREGNANCY

The use of any cured pork, even once per month, triples the risk of *toxoplasmosis,* which can cause miscarriage, fetal brain damage, or blindness.

Pregnant women who eat one or more pork hot dogs per week expose their unborn children to a 230% higher risk of brain tumors.

SKIN
The histamine content of pork fosters eczema and boils.

STOMACH
Salmonella is a type of bacterium that frequently causes serious gastroenteritis *[inflammation of stomach and intestine]*. Salmonella contaminates between 5–30% of swine carcasses in slaughterhouses. Many swine already have the bacteria in their gut upon entering. Only high temperature cooking can kill it. Barbeque heat is not hot enough according to the Center for Disease Control in Atlanta, Georgia.

Shellfish are very difficult to digest due to abundant collagen which slows the digestive juices. Shellfish cause poisoning, paralysis, diarrhea, nervous disorders and sometimes death. Ingestion of contaminated shellfish produces severe blood poisoning proving fatal in half of the cases. The following symptoms of food poisoning appear within 30 minutes of digestion of shellfish – a tingling sensation to facial area, headache, nausea, vomiting, numbness, paralysis of respiratory muscles and abdominal pain. Often times if the food is not ruled "contaminated" by health authorities the cause of death remains a mystery. Mice are used to inject tissue extracted from suspected shellfish to see whether they die. To be fighting gastritis or ulcers and eat shellfish is to reverse the healing process.

WARTS
Warts are common on the hands of butchers and slaughterhouse workers that handle pork and caused by the HPV-7 virus. It is found almost exclusively on the hands of those who handle raw meat and pork in particular. *Condylomas* are tumor-like growths of viral origin in the form of huge warts on the anus or external genitalia. There have been cases disappearing after giving up pork.

"PROOF" TEXTS REGARDING UNCLEAN FOODS

The 27 most popular Bible verses used to justify eating anything are examined in detail in this book.

"Every moving thing that liveth shall be meat for you; even as the green herb have I given you all things" (Gen. 9:1–3).

"Take no thought for your life, what ye shall eat, or what ye shall drink … Is not the life more than meat …" (Matt. 6:25).

"There is nothing from without a man, that entering into him can defile him: but the things which come out of him, those are they that defile the man" (Mark 7:14–16)

"Eat such things as are set before you ... And in the same house remain, eating and drinking such things as they give ..." (Luke 10:7, 8).

"Give alms of such things as ye have; and behold, all things are clean unto you" (Luke 11:41).

"What God hath cleansed, that call not thou common" (Acts 10:15).

"He that eateth, eateth to the Lord, for he giveth God thanks; and he that eateth not, to the Lord he eateth not, and giveth God thanks" (Rom. 14:6).

"But if thy brother be grieved with thy meat, now walkest thou not charitably. Destroy not him with thy meat ... Let not then your good be evil spoken of" (Rom. 14:13–16).

"I know, and am persuaded by the Lord Jesus, that there is nothing unclean of itself: but to him that esteemed any thing to be unclean to him it is unclean" (Rom. 14:14).

"For the kingdom of God is not meat and drink; but righteousness, and peace, and joy in the Holy Ghost ... Let us therefore follow after the things which make for peace, and things wherewith one may edify another. For meat destroy not the work of God" (Rom. 14:17, 19, 20).

"All things indeed are pure; but it is evil for that man who eateth with offence" (Rom. 14:20).

"Happy is he that condemneth not himself in that thing which he alloweth" (Rom. 14:22).

"And he that doubteth is damned if he eat, because he eateth not of faith: for whatsoever is not of faith is sin" (Rom. 14:23).

"But meat commendeth us not to God: for neither, if we eat, are we the better; neither, if we eat not, are we the worse" (1 Cor. 8:8).

"All things are lawful for me, but all things are not expedient: all things are lawful for me, but all things edify not" (1 Cor. 10:23).

"Whatsoever is sold in the shambles (the market) that eat ..." (1 Cor. 10:25).

"Asking no question for conscience sake" (1 Cor. 10:25).

"For the earth is the Lord's and the fullness thereof" (1 Cor. 10:26).

"If any of them that believe not bid you to a feast, and ye be disposed to go; whatsoever is set before you, eat, asking no question for conscience sake" (1 Cor. 10:27).

"For why is my liberty judged of another man's conscience? For if I by grace be a partaker, why am I evil spoken of for that for which I give thanks?" (1 Cor. 10:29, 30).

"Whether therefore ye eat, or drink, or whatsoever ye do, do all to the glory of God" (1 Cor. 10:31).

"Blotting out the handwriting of ordinances ... and took it out of the way, nailing it to His cross ... which are a shadow of things to come ..." (Col. 2:14, 17).

"Let no man therefore judge you in meat, or in drink, or in respect of an holy day, or of the new moon, or of the Sabbath days" (Col. 2:16).

"Wherefore, if ye be dead with Christ from the rudiments of the world, why as though living in the world, are ye subject to ordinances?" (Col. 2:20).

"Unto the pure all things are pure ..." (Titus 1:15).

"But unto them that are defiled and unbelieving is nothing pure ... they profess that they know God; but ... being abominable, and disobedient, and unto every good work reprobate" (Titus 1:15–16).

"Forbidding to marry and commanding to abstain from meats, which God hath created to be received with thanksgiving of them which believe and know the truth" (1 Tim. 4:2, 3).

"For every creature of God is good, and nothing to be refused, if it be received in thanksgiving. For it is sanctified by the word of God and prayer" (1 Tim. 4:4, 5).

TEACH Services, Inc.
P U B L I S H I N G

We invite you to view the complete
selection of titles we publish at:
www.TEACHServices.com

We encourage you to write us
with your thoughts about this,
or any other book we publish at:
info@TEACHServices.com

TEACH Services' titles may be purchased in
bulk quantities for educational, fund-raising,
business, or promotional use.
bulksales@TEACHServices.com

Finally, if you are interested in seeing
your own book in print, please contact us at:
publishing@TEACHServices.com

We are happy to review your manuscript at no charge.

www.ingramcontent.com/pod-product-compliance
Lightning Source LLC
Chambersburg PA
CBHW070558160426
43199CB00014B/2541